How We Behave
at the Feast

HOW WE BEHAVE AT THE FEAST

Reflections on Living in an Age of Plenty

DWIGHT CURRIE

Cliff Street Books
An Imprint of HarperCollinsPublishers

HarperCollins books may be purchased for educational, business, or sales promotional use. For information please write: Special Markets Department, HarperCollins Publishers Inc., 10 East 53rd Street, New York, NY 10022.

FIRST EDITION

Designed by Nancy B. Field

Printed on acid-free paper.

Library of Congress Cataloging-in-Publication Data

Currie, Dwight.
   How we behave at the feast : reflections on living in an age of plenty / Dwight Currie. — 1st ed.
       p.   cm.
    ISBN 0-06-019531-2
    1. Conduct of life.   I. Title.
   BJ1581.2.C88   2000
   170' .44—dc21   99-38737

---

00 01 02 03 04 ❖ / HC 10 9 8 7 6 5 4 3 2 1

In memory of my big brother, Daryl.

He taught me to laugh.

CONTENTS

JULY
Mind Your Manners

AUGUST
May I Be Excused?

SEPTEMBER
They Serve Who Also Wait

OCTOBER
Would You Like a Doggy Bag?

INTRODUCTION

*"He comes as a guest to the feast of existence,
and knows that what matters is not how much he inherits
but how he behaves at the feast,
and what people remember and love him for."*

—BORIS PASTERNAK, *To Friends East and West*

Are we having fun yet?

We should be.

We should be having great fun—or at least enjoying ourselves.

Never before in human history have so many of us luxuriated in pleasures once reserved only for royalty. Look at the comforts, the conveniences, the cars, and the clothes. Think of the leisure, the travel, the arts, and the culture we enjoy. We have arrived, as Boris Pasternak once said, "as guests at the feast of existence."

So I ask once again: "Are we having fun yet?"

Why not? What's wrong?

Why all the anxiety? Why all the bitterness and confusion? Why the dread? Why the envy, the fear, the greed and hostility? Why this alphabet soup of indigestion as we belly up to a buffet of unprecedented bounty? What's the problem?

It's us. We have forgotten our manners. We care too much about what we can get—*how much we inherit*—and too little about how we *behave*. It's as simple as that.

In our shortsighted quest for our share, we've become abrupt (if not outright rude), aggressive (which is a nice way of saying pushy), insistent, and insensitive. We demand, we grab, we elbow our way to the front of the line, and if we part with some cash, we believe our social sins are forgiven. But it's never enough.

Even when our pockets are empty, the cupboards of our desires are not yet full. We begrudgingly go to work, only to earn more money—and the cycle of our bad behavior spirals ever higher. We call it the rat race, but that's unfair to the rats! Rats are, by nature, scavengers. Rats *have to* crawl and fight their way through the garbage in order to eat and survive. We do not.

Think about this the next time you're fuming in the slow-moving line at the grocery store. Take a look in your cart. It's full. So is the cart in front of you and so is the one behind you. You all have what you need. So what's the problem?

"I'm going to be late!" you cry. "They should have more clerks!" someone else declares. And you're probably right. However, in less than thirty minutes you'll be on your way home. Mission accomplished. You didn't have to kill any rats to get tonight's dinner, so why were you such a rat to everyone around you? Is it because it feels good to huff and puff your way into a self-righteous outrage? There's no excuse. Except to say, "We have forgotten our manners."

Well, it's time to remember our manners. It's time to reflect on how we behave at the feast.

Of all the pleasures we enjoy, our greatest luxury is the freedom to choose. We have a choice about how we behave, and that means we have the choice to opt for civility and grace.

That's what this book is about. It was inspired by an essay by Boris Pasternak in which he voiced his hope for the youth of the post World War II era. One passage in particular stuck with me:

> . . . he comes as a guest to the feast of existence, and
> knows that whatmatters is not how much he inherits,
> but how he behaves at the feast, and what people
> remember and love him for.

I underlined that passage, read it again, and then I thought to myself: "How do *I* behave at the feast?" I had no answer at the time, but the question continued to haunt me.

It was some time later when I got my answer. You see, I used to behave like a rat in the grocery store. One day, as I was sighing and griping and demanding to know "Why aren't there more clerks?"—I turned and snarled at an elderly man who accidentally bumped me in the butt with his shopping cart. When I saw my self-absorbed rudeness reflected in his injured eyes, I heard a voice inside my head: "How are you behaving at the feast?" I was almost paralyzed with shame. I mumbled an apology and offered a timid smile. That question resulted in some serious attitude adjustment.

I began to put the question to friends as well, and often

it led to some lively and enlightening discussions. They would ask:

"How do you know we're even invited?"

"What's on the menu?"

"Do I have to bring anything?"

"Who else is going to be there?"

"Will I have to wait tables?"

"It is black tie?"

The answers to those questions—and to many more—form the basis for the reflections that follow. Each is a reminder, a suggestion, a warning, or a reprimand—and each asks the same question: "How are we behaving at the feast?"

The book follows the calendar year and uses the seasons, the holidays, some folklore, and cultural events as the starting points to explore the ways we can celebrate our existence. January advances the theme of the feast. February explores who's invited. March focuses on what's being served. April reminds us that we are all April Fools; May deals with our lot in life; and June examines our response to that lot. July reminds us to "mind our manners," and August looks at those times when we'd rather be alone. September extols the dignity of work; October covers harvest; November is all about gratitude; and December's theme is acceptance.

You can start at the beginning and read one each week or you can start in the middle and pick and choose as you please. But before you go on, take a moment to read Pasternak's passage one more time. This time, rephrase the question slightly and ask yourself, "How am I—*as a guest*—behaving at the Feast of Existence?"

There are three key words in this question:

1. *Guest:* defined by Webster's as "a visitor."

2. *Feast:* "a celebration of abundance and richness."

3. *Behave:* "conduct oneself in the correct or proper way."

If you interject these definitions into the question, you get: "How am I—a visitor—behaving? Am I conducting myself in the correct and proper way at this wonderful celebration of abundance and richness we call life? Am I having fun yet?"

Remember, you always have a choice.

As Henry David Thoreau once wrote, "To affect the quality of the day, that is the highest of arts." We can master that artistry by always remembering that it is our *behavior* that we, visitors to this planet, will ultimately be remembered and loved for. This book was written to remind us of that. A friend calls it: "Table manners for the soul."

Welcome to the Feast, and *Bon Appétit!*

JANUARY

Life Is a Banquet!

*"A man is rich in proportion to
the number of things
which he can afford to let alone."*

—HENRY DAVID THOREAU

What Are You Waiting for, an Engraved Invitation?

THERE'S A WONDERFUL OLD FOLKTALE about a school of very intellectual fish. They met one day to discuss the belief that all fish had life, breathed, and took their existence from one source: The Water. Water was everything—yet not one of them knew what water actually was. No one had ever seen it. How did they know it existed?

Their discussion became quite impassioned, and one fish cautioned, "Let's not ask questions, let's just believe." But a bigger fish insisted, "How can we believe in water if we don't even know what water is?" A third fish opined, "Maybe water is a state of mind." "Maybe water is love," said a fourth. The fifth and smallest among them suggested they go to the Ancient Fish for the answer.

The five fish swam for days and days, upstream and downstream, through the lakes, into the rivers, and out into the ocean until they found the wise old fish. "What is water?" they wanted to know.

"What *isn't* water?" the wise one replied. "If you can show me one thing that isn't water," she said, "then I might be able to answer your question. But, it's *all* in the water."

For days, those fish had been swimming around looking for water. It wasn't until the old fish said, "You're soaking in it right now!" that they finally understood.

The Feast of Existence represents the same problem for

3

a lot of people. "Where is this feast?" they want to know. "How do we know it exists?" "Is it simply a state of mind?" "What's being served?"

I think the wise fish would say, "It's *all* a feast. You're soaking in it right now!" Look around you. Your home, your family, your friends, your health, your mind, the trees, the music, the poetry, the art, the sunshine—all in all, it is quite a feast.

Maybe not everything is exactly to your liking. Perhaps some of it is bitter and almost impossible to swallow. There are certainly times when it seems as if this feast serves up nothing but lima bean casseroles, but for the most part, Mother Nature puts out quite a spread.

My own mother put out quite a spread, too. Many nights, after she had called us to the table three or four times, she would lose her patience, step out of the kitchen, and demand to know, "What are you waiting for, an engraved invitation?"

Her question required no answer except action. Within seconds, we were all at the table. The feast was before us.

The Feast of Existence is all around you. It's a big, bounteous (sometimes messy and chaotic) celebration of all the confusing abundance and varied richness that life has to offer. Why be a fish out of water? Why swim around aimlessly asking yourself, "What is life? What is happiness?"

Why wait for Mother Nature to lose her patience before you come to the table? Do you need death and disaster to remind you of how precious life is?

What *are* you waiting for?

At the start of a new year, please accept this book as your engraved invitation to the Feast of Existence. It's an invitation to abandon all the excuses you've made for staying away, an invitation to assume your share of the responsibilities for making the feast a success, and an invitation to reexamine your attitude about what's on the table and about the people who are seated there with you.

I invite you to consider all the choices: To feast or famine—to share or shirk—to accept or reject. You have those choices. When making your decisions, always remember that you come as a guest and what matters most is *how you behave at the feast.*

How you choose to behave is what people will remember and love you for.

The Watched Pot

ALEXANDER POPE once suggested we add a ninth beatitude that would read: "Blessed is the man who expects nothing, for he shall never be disappointed."

Expectations. They're dangerous things—and we all have them. Expectations for ourselves, for our spouses, and for our children. Expectations of love and happiness and success. We hope, and plan, and pave life's road with these good intentions—and all along the way our expectations lead us down a hell-bound route to disappointment.

Think of the child who expects a pony for Christmas and is disappointed with the puppy he receives instead. Or the wife who can't smell the roses because she's always expecting the diamonds. Or the man who expects to earn millions, then suffers a heart attack at mid-life when he has only one—million, that is. Expectations do that. They doom you to desire a life that might be, by blinding you to the life that you have.

That is, by definition, what it means to expect. It is from the Latin *spectare*—to see. If "spectare" is to see, then to "exspectare" is to stop seeing. We stop seeing because we're forever expecting—forever watching the pot that never boils. We end up hot, frustrated, and stewing alone in the kitchen of expectations while everyone else is partying at the feast.

So, how do we keep our expectations in check? How do we avoid a life of disappointment?

I'm going to suggest that it's simply a matter of opening

our eyes—to take the "ex" out of "expect" and to "spectare," *to see,* to look at the feast in some different ways instead. Here are my suggestions, in alphabetical order:

- Whenever we find we are dissatisfied with our jobs or our spouses or our houses or our life, we have to remember that we are seeing only an *as*pect—one view—one part of the feast.

- At these times, we need to be more *circum*spect—to look around.

- We need to *in*spect what we do have.

- When we take a close look and count our blessings, the *pro*spects improve and life starts to look good again.

- It's only when we give our lives *another* look, when we give ourselves and each other the *re*spect we deserve, that we can finally see just how *spectacular* the Feast of Existence really is. We just have to open our eyes to see it.

That's what the British writer G. K. Chesterton did. He took Alexander Pope's ninth beatitude and put a more optimistic twist on it: "Blessed is he that expecteth nothing, for he shall be gloriously surprised."

I much prefer surprises to expectations and disappointments. Surprises are so much more fun.

Take birthday parties, for example. Imagine the potential for disappointment if you walked into a room and everyone jumped out and shouted "Expect!" What could possibly follow that? Isn't it better to have a glorious "Surprise!"?

Expectations are seldom met, but life is—it's usually met head-on, and seldom do you get what you expected.

Yes, I know you expected New York to be a lot cleaner, but isn't it surprisingly lively and fun?

I'm sorry your flight was delayed for six hours, but weren't you surprised to make a new friend?

I'm sure it was disappointing when your daughter dropped out of medical school, but what a wonderful surprise to have a rodeo clown in the family!

When we welcome life with gratitude and respect, when we turn away from our expectations and look around at what we already have, then our unwatched pot suddenly starts to boil over with possibilities. Then, the Feast of Existence becomes a glorious surprise.

Stop *expecting* it and start *seeing* it.

Come as You Are

HAVE YOU EVER WONDERED why Cinderella's shoe didn't disappear? Everything else did; the dress, the tiara, even the hairdo—*poof!* All gone at the stroke of midnight. So why not the shoe? Why was that glass slipper still there when all else had vanished?

Let's start at the beginning, for Cinderella has much to teach us about how to behave at the feast.

To begin, it's important to note that everyone is invited to the ball—including Cinderella. The reasons she uses for not going to the party are two of the oldest excuses in the book: "I've got too much to do," and "I don't have a thing to wear." I know the traditional interpretation is to blame the wicked stepwomen in Cinderella's life, (and we'll get to them in a minute) but for now, while everyone else is at the feast, our heroine is overworked, underdressed, and sitting alone in the kitchen at her own private pity party. Poor Cinderella, all alone with nothing to eat except the bitter regrets of "if only" and the sweet dreams of "I wish."

Next scene: Enter Fairy Godmother—and *poof!*—it's rags to riches, peasant to princess, pumpkins to Porsches. Cinderella is looking good, she's feeling good, and she's on her way to the ball. There's only one catch: It won't last—there's a curfew. But for now, it doesn't matter—Cinderella is in a happy place. She's at the palace, she's the belle of the ball, and the evil stepsisters (those models out of *Vogue*) are green with envy.

This is justice. If only she could let them know who she really is. But she can't, because Cinderella is in disguise. She's not a real princess at all. When the bell starts to toll, her mask starts to slip, the seams start to split, and the coif starts to fall. The jig is up. She's about to be exposed!

She makes a run for it, and in her haste she loses a shoe. There's no time to look back now. She goes galumphing into the night, back to the kitchen and the ashes. No one will ever know. Her dream has ended. Who did she think she was anyway?

Except—the shoe didn't disappear! When everything else had vanished, that shoe was still there for the Prince to find. With that shoe, the Prince tracks her down and the rest of their story is "happily ever after."

So, what do we think we have learned?

- Worrying about work and wardrobe can keep us from the party. *True.*

- We can go to the ball only if we have the right clothes. With the right outfit, we can leave a good impression (or in Cinderella's case, a shoe) and eventually we will be singled out, tracked down, and rewarded for our great virtue. *Maybe.*

- All we need is a Fairy Godmother. *Please, grow up!*

Fairy Godmothers exist only in fairy tales, and without a Fairy Godmother you're back to sitting alone in the kitchen. So what's a potential princess to do?

Go back to the beginning. Remember, the invitation has your name on it—and, if you look closely, you will see that it says, "Come as You Are!" You have that choice.

If you choose to let fashion and fatigue keep you from the festivities, then fine, sit in the ashes, blame your family for everything, and spend all your time and money scratching lottery tickets with the hope that a Fairy Godmother might someday come to your rescue.

Or, you can pick yourself up, dust yourself off, and fly to the party like a phoenix. Now, here I'm going to suggest a substitute for Cinderella: *Martha Stewart.* That's right, a real Cinderella for the twenty-first century. You may recall that Martha started out in the kitchen, too. She wasn't invited to the parties, she catered them. Maybe Martha discovered that tears shed into the ashes created something that could be used as mascara! In any case, that girl became the belle of the ball! And you can, too.

So, here are the real lessons to learn:

- The Feast of Existence is open to everyone—regardless of career or couture.

- The impression you make is as illusive and as fragile as Cinderella's glass slipper, so make sure it fits. Don't go pretending to be something you're not and you'll never have to leave the party in panic and disguise.

- Don't wait for a Fairy Godmother—or for anyone else—to validate your ticket to the feast. Make your own style.

Which brings us back to the shoes.

Cinderella's shoe didn't vanish because *it* was still in that enchanted place where Cinderella was at her best. She behaved very well at the feast, but she lost her nerve—her self-confidence. She ran. Just as some people leave their hearts in San Francisco, Cinderella left one shoe in a place where her dreams never disappear.

And what happened to the other shoe? My theory is that Cinderella was still wearing it when she got home. Without thinking, she kicked it off and lost it in the back of her closet, where it was forgotten until the Prince came along with its mate.

This may have worked for Cinderella, but if I were you, I wouldn't wait for Prince Charming to knock at my door with one-half of my lost dreams. I'd dig through that closet of old desires, try on a few for size, and if the fantasy fits—wear it to the feast.

Come as you are—or come as you want to be. But . . . come.

Make Yourself at Home!

AT THIS POINT you might be asking yourself: "If we're all *guests* at the Feast of Existence, then who is the *host*? Who is responsible for this great celebration of life?"

These are questions with no easy answers. But they are questions made up of words. Often, if we really understand what it is that we are asking, we find the answers in the words of the questions.

So, Question #1: "If we're all *guests*, then who is the *host*?"

Let's turn to the *American Heritage Dictionary* for help on this one. The definition of *guest* is: "one to whom hospitality is given by a host," and the definition of *host* is: "one who receives or entertains guests."

Dictionaries are notorious for leading us into mazes of self-referential definitions. But in this case, it leads right to the heart of the question; for the relationship between a guest and a host is a very circuitous affair indeed. If you look again at the definitions for *guest* and *host,* you will find the same rather cryptic note at the end of both entries. It reads: "See *ghos-ti* in Appendix." That's where you'll find the answer!

In the language of our ancient Indo-European ancestors there was a wonderful word: *ghos-ti*. *Ghos-ti* meant "host"—and—*ghos-ti* meant "guest." Host and Guest. Guest and Host. *Ghos-ti*. One word. One in the same

15

thing. As the entry elaborates: *ghos-ti* is "someone with whom one has reciprocal duties of hospitality."

So, there's the answer to Question #1: "If we're all guests, then we're also all hosts." We're all in this together, with "reciprocal duties of hospitality"—meaning:

1. Reciprocal: "given or owed to each other."

2. Duties: "moral obligations."

3. Hospitality: "cordial and generous reception."

We're not simply a guest, nor are we the host. We're both! We're something very old—yet maybe something very new. We're *ghos-ti*. We're celebrants at the Feast of Existence, morally obliged to receive one another with warmth, sincerity, and generosity. That's a tall order, and it's not an easy answer, but it's the only way the feast can go on.

Now, Question #2: "Who is responsible for this great celebration of life?"

The answer should be apparent: "We are! The *ghos-ti*. All of us together."

I can best illustrate the nature of *ghos-ti* by sharing a personal story.

A few years ago I arrived at a friend's home at the onset of a weeklong visit. He greeted me at the door with a hearty, "Welcome! Make yourself at home!" I thanked him and assured him that I would indeed be comfortable. In response he elaborated, "My house is your house!" So again, I thanked him for his hospitality—and again he upped the ante. "My kitchen is your kitchen," he said, and before I could reply, his welcome continued: "My grocery store is your grocery store," he explained, "my stove is your stove, my dishwasher is your dishwasher, my broom is your broom." He stopped, grinned at me, and asked, "Do you get the idea?" I nodded.

The distinction between host and guest had been blurred. Yes, I was truly welcome to his hospitality, but I was also expected to reciprocate, to take care of myself, and to do my share. It was one of the most liberating welcomes I ever received. Not once during my visit did I feel as if I was imposing, and the time we spent together was so mutually gratifying that my friend and I frequently come as guests to one another's home. That's *ghos-ti!*

There is one final challenge.

In addition to meaning both *host* and *guest, ghos-ti* is also the word for *stranger.* That's right: Host, Guest, *and* Stranger. That's everyone—and anyone—with whom one has reciprocal duties of hospitality.

That makes the answer much harder and the challenge even greater. We must not only welcome our friends, family, and neighbors to the feast, but also those strangers we meet there. I'm sorry, but those are the rules of the *ghos-ti.*

It's not enough to say to our friends, "My feast is your feast." We must—with those friends—also say, "It's his feast and her feast and their feast—and everyone's feast."

We must be willing to say to everyone, "Make yourself at home!"

Take All You Want,
but Eat All You Take

WHEN YOU STEP UP to the buffet line at a popular all-you-can-eat restaurant in my hometown, you are greeted with the following sign: "Take all you want, but eat all you take."

This is not so much an *invitation* as it is a *warning*—a potential reprimand for gluttony.

Bountiful eateries like this can be found in small towns all over America's heartland. They are joyous places where predominantly agrarian communities gather to celebrate their vital role in filling the Breadbasket of the World. It's not uncommon for someone near the end of the line to shout out good-naturedly to those filling their plates in front of him, "Hey, leave a little there for the rest of us!" This always elicits a general communal guffaw, for they know there is little chance of shortage. There always will be plenty to eat at the all-you-can-eat buffet.

So, please—"Take all you want."

But—"Eat all you take!"

Once, as a child, I bellied up to the buffet and heaped my plate so full that it became apparent I would fail to comply with the proprietor's posted directive. As the rest of my family completed their meals, I still faced a mountain of food. My grandfather admonished me by asking, "Were your eyes bigger than your belly?" I nodded, hoping that my confession would excuse me from cleaning my plate, but he waited, and eventually I did eat all that I had taken. I left the table with a clear conscience, and also with a miserable stomachache. I had learned one of the fundamental lessons of the feast: "Gluttony is its own punishment." You can't celebrate, sing, or sleep with an overstuffed stomach.

So why, as our bellies grow so big, do our eyes continue to grow bigger still? Why do we keep heaping on more and more and more *stuff*? Why must we have everything we see? Our closets are full, our attics are full, our basements and garages—even our highways—are lined with unsightly rows of self-storage units. What's it all for?

There's an old Jewish saying that gives us the answer: "Where there is too much, something is missing."

I once read about a fabulously wealthy woman and her many, many mansions, chateaux, villas, and estates. She had houses scattered here and abroad, but few were ever seen or used by the owner. It was at one such palatial country estate that she greeted her guests with a sweeping gesture and said, "Welcome! It's not home, but it is *much*!"

There, in the midst of much *muchness*, something was missing. She had many houses, but she had no home. She couldn't celebrate, or sing, or sleep either, and I believe she eventually ended her life in suicide. A grim story—but true.

Everywhere we look we see commercial messages that urge us to want more, to buy more, to take more. They block our vision even as they make our eyes grow wider with desire; eyes that not only grow bigger than our bellies, but often bigger than our bank accounts, too. What is missing that we should want so much? What can't we see?

We can't see the scenery because we have built storage

units. We can't smell the roses because we seldom find time to set foot in the garden. We can't pay the piper because we're too far in debt. And we can't roll up the rug for dancing because there's too much damn furniture on it!

As we come to the Feast of Existence, it's good to remember the words of the sixteenth-century British writer John Heywood: "Enough is as good as a feast."

Any more than that leads to heartburn.

FEBRUARY

Guess Who's Coming to Dinner

"Above all we need, particularly as children, the reassuring presence of a visible community, an intimate group that enfolds us with understanding and love . . ."

—LEWIS MUMFORD

It Depends on How You Look at It

IT'S TIME TO RETHINK Groundhog Day.

Traditionally, it's assumed that should the furry fore-caster emerge from his winter's rest and see his shadow, he will scurry back into his den and stay there, hibernating deep underground while the rest of us endure yet another six weeks of winter. Conversely, if he doesn't see his shadow, he will happily hurry forth as a harbinger of spring, and we will all rejoice with him as he ends his long, cold fast. Spring will be here in about—well, *six weeks*.

There you have it. Either way, it's always the same. It's either six more weeks of winter, or it's only six more weeks until spring. It depends on how you look at it—or more to the point, it depends on how the *groundhog* looks at it.

You see, it's not a question of whether or not the sun is shining on February 2. What really matters on that day is which way the groundhog is *looking* when he crawls out of his hole. It's the sight of his shadow—not the sun—that sends him back underground. Shadows are scary, and that's why Mr. G. stays in bed with the covers over his head.

On the other hand, if he peers out and feels the warmth of the sun on his face, his shadow is cast *behind* him and he ventures forth with confidence that spring is just around the corner. One way he spends six more weeks hibernating in a hole—the other way he hungrily rejoins us at the Feast of Existence. (Yes, groundhogs are invited, too.)

There are a lot of shadows that can keep us from the feast.

In a culture that grows increasingly more violent, many of us are afraid to walk the city streets, hesitant to travel the nation's highways, and terrified to board an international flight. Families are torn apart by petty jealousies and feuds, and the marketplace is crowded, noisy, and ultimately unsatisfying. We become angry and afraid, tired and unsure. We see these shadows and head underground.

Now, I'm not going to suggest to you that it's simply a matter of looking the other way. We can't ignore all the shadows—we can't deny all the darkness. Those who try eventually become like Peter Pan, who, when he lost *his* shadow, triumphantly announced, "I won't grow up!" Living in Never Never Land is as futile as hibernating in a hole.

But, it's good to remember that most shadows disappear when we turn on the lights. Fears can be overcome when we face them head-on. Anger can be defused. Hurts can be healed. Rest can be won. We can turn our faces to the sun and in the light of day be confident that we are stronger than our shadows.

It's hard sometimes. Always looking at the sun can blind us to reality, but it simply depends on how you look at it. We have choices. We can hide under the covers or face the day. Either way, the shadows still exist. We can choose between six long weeks—or a lifetime—lost to fear, or six short weeks—or a lifetime—devoted to finding some solutions.

Here's what I suggest we do. Each year on February 2, instead of casting our fate to the groundhog, I think we should look up to the sun. We should note how it moves ever higher in the sky. We should watch as each day it rises a little earlier and lingers a moment longer. We should know that the Earth keeps turning, and the dance with the sun continues just as it should. If we emulate that dance, and *trust* in that dance, we will find—in time—that the sun sheds its light and brings its warmth even to the darkest of corners.

There's no place you can hibernate forever. Eventually, you have to step out and join us at the feast. What you find here, be it sunshine or shadow, friends or foes, feast or famine, fun or fear, largely depends on you.

It depends on how you look at it.

"Be Mine"
Or, the Question of How Many
Valentines to Send

I'VE NEVER UNDERSTOOD the commercial slogan that reads: "When you care enough to send the very best." It seems to imply there are other occasions when you care enough only to send something mediocre. That really puts the *sin* in in*sin*cere, and that is the reason I'm always a little uncomfortable with Valentine's Day.

It all began in grade school. Every year it was understood that you would bring a Valentine for every classmate, and in turn every classmate would bring a Valentine for you. We decorated shoe boxes to serve as receptacles.

The week before the big day, my mother purchased an assortment of Valentines from the Five and Dime, and I proceeded to make my selections. First, I chose the very best, the prettiest card, for my teacher. Then, I picked the next best greeting for my secret sweetheart. I worked my way through the list of classmates, sending the better Valentines to my friends, and foisting the lesser cards on my enemies. Always (and here, I now must make a terrible confession) I picked the ugliest Valentine for a girl we'll call Sheila. I did this every year.

Everybody had a Sheila in his or her classroom. She was the girl who was too tall, a little overweight, not so smart, and far from pretty. I always feared that Sheila secretly liked me, so I protected myself by sending her my very worst. It still shames me to remember this. But, such are the sins you inevitably commit when you try to send Valentines to everyone.

Yes, everyone is invited to the feast. And everyone should feel welcome, at home, and everyone should receive a Valentine from someone. But not necessarily from me.

It is natural—and good—that we should have special friends, close family ties, and especially that one most beloved person in our lives. These people form the inner circle of love and support to which we can turn in good times and in bad. It is to this circle we should send our very best, and it is from this circle we seek to draw the same from others.

Beyond that circle lies our communities, our nations, and our world. As compassionate as we may want to be, there are far too many people on Earth to include them all in our innermost circle of caring. When we say we *love* everyone on Earth, it's a lot like sending an ugly Valentine to Sheila—it just doesn't ring true. You know it, and so does she.

Being sappy and saccharine in our rhetoric will not protect us from the moral obligation to be cordial and generous in our actions.

We must allow everyone to dance in a circle of their own making—no matter how dissonant the music is to our ears. We must acknowledge whatever love they find there—no matter how different it is from our own. We must accept the happiness that lives there—no matter how it might elude our understanding, and we must honor those lives as we honor our own. This is much harder than sending our second-best Valentines, for it demands something better than cheap sentiments and empty platitudes. It requires us to send our *very* best—our tolerance and our respect.

I recently heard that Sheila grew up to be a schoolteacher. I'd like to think that schoolboys are sending their best Valentines to her. In any case, Sheila doesn't need to receive anything more from me, but I'd like her to know that I've grown up enough to wish her the very best.

May I See Your Invitation?

HAVE YOU EVER given much thought to the word *club*?

Isn't it interesting that we use the same word to describe a weapon that we use to define those organizations that meet behind closed doors—doors on which it is written "Members Only"? I've always been a little nervous around clubs—both kinds.

A club is lethal when it's used as a weapon to keep someone out. The whole history of the world can be told in the tragic conflicts of class, caste, race, religion, gender, apartheid, and genocide. Yet still, "exclusive" is one of the most seductive and dangerous words that we wield at the Feast of Existence. It starts with something as simple as "No Girls Allowed," but it can lead in the end to a holocaust.

Why must belonging necessitate exclusion? Why must someone be kept out in order for the rest of us to want in? And for that matter, is inclusion any better? If to "exclude" someone is to shut him out, then to "include" someone is to shut him in. Membership in the wrong club might be worse than no membership at all. Either way, when you're a club-carrying member, your world grows smaller and your options become fewer. As Groucho Marx was known to say, "I don't want to belong to any club that will accept me for a member."

There will always be those who opt to live inside exclusive worlds, walled away from the rest of us. To assure themselves that they are happy there, they do their best to convince *us* that the grass is very much greener on their side of the fence. They make it sound so inviting, yet when we arrive at their gate someone is there to ask, "May I see your invitation?" That is the time to turn and walk away from all the gates and the walls.

We have an invitation to the Feast of Existence—we don't need an entrée to anything else.

The great American poet Robert Frost understood walls. In his famous poem titled "Mending Wall," two neighbors work together to rebuild the wall that marks the common boundary of their properties. As they labor, the poet wonders why they even need the wall. After all, on his side there is an apple orchard and on the neighbor's side there is a pine grove. Apples and pinecones do not need fences. The neighbor replies with one of the most famous lines in all of poetry: "Good fences make good neighbors."

The poet considers this answer, but still questions the value of the wall—this time wondering just what is being walled *in* and what is being walled *out*. And again the neighbor says: "Good fences make good neighbors."

Now, it's easy to conclude from this poem that Frost believed walls were a necessary prerequisite to neighborhood peace. But, just as it's dangerous to exclude and to include, when you *conclude* too quickly, you shut out thought.

I don't think Frost saw that wall as keeping anything *out* or anything *in*. That wall brought those two neighbors *together* in an annual ritual of self-definition and mutual regard. It is, after all, a *mending* wall, and that is what

Frost understood. The neighbors did not build the wall in order to stay apart, but to come together. Coming together is what made them good neighbors—not staying apart.

It's okay to have boundaries. It's okay to have pinecones while another has an apple orchard. It's even okay to have a wall that marks the point where you begin and where your neighbor leaves off. However, once you build that wall so high that neither you nor your neighbor can see, step, or leap over it, well—then you have the beginnings of a problem. The next thing you know, you'll be looking for a club.

Once, as I was about to land at the small airport in Sioux City, Iowa, the farm fields of the great mid-western plains rose up to greet me. A mother behind me commented to her child, "Doesn't it look like a big patchwork quilt?" This oft-repeated observation was by now a cliché, and yet I had to agree that those fields of corn and oats and beans and grass do indeed come together in a most pleasing way. As we neared the ground, I saw the fences that separate those fields, and I thought of Robert Frost's poem. Those fences give no offense to anyone. They are not rips in the landscape but rather great seams where the fabric of our heartland is forever stitched together.

When we finally touched back down on Earth, I knew no one would be there to ask, "May I see your invitation?" I was already a member.

I didn't need a club to get in.

Spacious Accommodations

IS YOUR TABLE starting to feel a little crowded? Are there too many people to seat and not enough places to put them? Is there too much to do and not enough time to do it in?

Don't panic. It happens to everyone. In fact, here's a little secret you probably learned in grade school but have since forgotten: Even the Earth is running late. That's right—every day it takes Mother Earth twenty-four hours and almost one full extra minute to finish her rotation around the sun. By the end of the year, she is five hours, forty-eight minutes, and forty-six seconds late. But do you ever get the sense that the Earth is in a hurry? Do you ever doubt that she finds time and space to accommodate us all? How does she do it?

Simple. She ignores the clock. She doesn't give the clock the time of day.

We're the ones who invented the clock. We're the ones who invented time and calendars and schedules. We're the ones who invented *late* and delays. As long ago as 200 B.C., the Greek writer Plautus complained: "Confound him who in this place set up a sundial, to cut and hack my days so wretchedly into small portions." *We* invented frustration.

In the meantime, the Earth doesn't concern herself with hours and minutes and schedules. She just keeps rollin' along, and in doing so has time for everything under the sun.

How can we be more like the Earth?

We need to accommodate our own limitations the same way we accommodate Mother Earth's chronic tardy behavior. Think about it. Does anyone ever complain about that extra minute she takes every day? Does anyone even notice the five hours, forty-eight minutes, and forty-six seconds every year? No. We just go about our lives. That's because we know that once every four years we will simply add a day to February and everything will be fine. Tardiness forgiven. It's our great *Leap to Accommodate*. And we don't have much choice, do we? No one is going to make the Earth spin any faster than she already does. The important thing to remember is that we're all spinning with her, and I repeat: We need to accommodate our own limitations the same way we accommodate the Earth's rotation.

Here're my suggestions:

1. Every day you must find one minute all for yourself. In the first thirty seconds, write down every petty annoyance, every little human imperfection, and every minor disturbance that has crowded your day and robbed you of time. Time's up. In the second thirty seconds, try to imagine who has listed *you* and your behavior on *their* roster of complaints. You still have fifteen seconds to go.

2. File these lists in a folder marked "Things to take care of on February 29."

3. Then, forget about it. Get on with your life.

4. The next time February 29 comes around, open the file and spend an entire day fussing and fuming and fretting about all of those terrible frustrations.

5. On March 1 everything will be fine. All will be forgiven.

I realize this means every February 29 is going to be very unpleasant. Everyone will be going around griping and complaining and casting stones. And dodging them. On the other hand, for every February 29 we will have 1,460 days of patience, tolerance, and compassion. It seems a fair trade. What's more, I bet most of us will open our file folders on February 29 and not even remember what all of those complaints were about. We will have made a great leap to accommodate our humanity.

Accommodate is a great word. It means to "make fit, to adjust or adapt. To reconcile differences. To do a service or a favor. To have space for."

Do yourself a favor—accommodate your limitations. Adjust to unexpected circumstances. Adapt to unanticipated frustrations. Reconcile the differences you have with the guests at your table. And, most important, have space and time for everyone and everything that life has to offer.

If this mean you'll be running five hours, forty-eight minutes, and forty-six seconds behind schedule, don't panic. The Feast is open twenty-four hours (and one extra minute) every day.

MARCH

What's on the Menu?

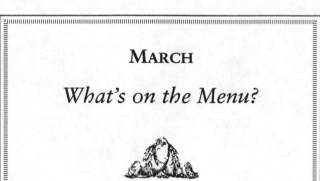

*"Unlimited opportunities
can be as potent a cause of frustration
as a paucity or lack of opportunities."*

—ERIC HOFFER

Are You Ready to Order?

WHAT ARE YOU going to say when the waiter comes to the table and asks, "Are you ready to order? Do you know what you'd like?"

Choices—always choices—we have a dizzying array of choices. From the first time someone asks, "What do you want to be when you grow up?" we are confronted with a lifetime of making choices: friends, career, marriage, politics, religion. And those are just the big ones. What about fashions and vacations and cars and long-distance telephone service? It's enough to make your head spin. And always, as you're trying to make up your mind, there is someone who is waiting and wanting to know: "Are you ready to order? Do you know what you'd like?"

The Feast of Existence offers the full menu of life's possibilities. It's all here—all the people, all the places, all the jobs and endeavors, all the hopes and the dreams. So where do you start? With something simple? Or do you move directly to a casserole of hype, hot spots, and holidays? There's a fine selection of music, of art, of romance—or would you prefer a quiet hobby, a little reading, a day of solitude, or a night of fun? From Adventure to "Z-z-z . . ." It's all here. Do you know what you'd like?

Life comes served in any order, any combination, or in any way you can possibly imagine. Sometimes the results are delicious, and sometimes it can be downright distasteful. That is the promise and the peril of a life filled with choices. Every day, every week, every minute of every year—we have choices. Are you ready to order?

I've found the best way to make life's choices is to reduce the menu to three basic options: Breakfast—Lunch—or Dinner.

What am I hungry for? Something new, something to *renew*, or am I ready for a snooze?

What time is it? Is it time to rise, to energize, or to celebrate before closing my eyes?

These are my three basic choices: Breakfast—Lunch—or Dinner. Once I know what I hunger for, the choices are easier to make.

For a long time, Breakfast was the most appealing meal of my life. I was always hungry for fresh starts—for new jobs, new cities, new adventures. Whenever the spirit moved me, I moved on to something different. Consequently, mine has been a rich and varied feast, but not one without days of indigestion. Always eating on the go leads to heartburn—and also to heart*ache*. Every time we opt for something new, something old gets left behind. A steady diet of breakfasts comes served with a lot of "good-byes"—so make sure you're hungry for both before placing your order.

As I've grown older (and maybe a little wiser), my taste for the new has been replaced with a hunger for *re*new. When life's diet seems boring and bland, I don't automatically call it quits and order up a whole new meal. I opt instead to renew, to refuel, and to reenergize. That's what Lunch is for—a chance to sit back, to think about where I've been and to dream about where I'm going. After a little rest and reflection, I'm ready to start up again right where I left off.

If it looks like the choices are few, that's the best time to order a Lunch. Too many people skip lunch; they mistake momentary fatigue for total exhaustion. A lot of "good-byes" could be "see ya later" if people took time for Lunch. Give yourself—or your family—or your marriage—or your job—a break now and then. Take a long walk, a short vacation, a day all alone, or an evening with friends.

Then, you have the option of Dinner—to celebrate a job well done, to join with family and friends at the end of a hectic day, or maybe to dine alone and to ready yourself for a period of much-needed rest. Opting for Dinner means you're hungry for reward. You should never go starved for a pat on the back or a feather in your cap; it's nice to be recognized for a job well done. Just remember, sometimes you have to pick up the check for *this* meal yourself. So if you're hungry for Dinner, don't hesitate to treat yourself to a feast. Going to bed without Dinner is one of life's most bitter punishments.

So—Are you ready to order? Do you know what you'd like?

Breakfast—Lunch—or Dinner?

Throughout our lives, we are granted these three choices—call them your three wishes: to start a new journey, to rest along the way, or to celebrate your safe return back home. Knowing where you are on the road of life is the best way of knowing what you'd like from the Feast of Existence.

That's the Way the Cookie Crumbles

SINCE TIME BEGAN we have yearned to take a sneak peak into the future—to catch just a glimpse at what fortune and follies tomorrow may bring. Some people read palms, others make star charts, a few search the tea leaves, and teenagers ask Ouija. There are those who look to the cards for the answers, and those who gaze into crystal balls.

My personal favorites are the sweet surrenders we make to the divinational powers of our desserts. Now I ask you, are there really such things as *just* desserts? Has anyone found *proof* in his or her simple bowl of pudding? Do birthday wishes depend on lungs large enough to extinguish the candles on our cake?

And, how can you be certain you are getting the fortune cookie that was truly intended for you?

Think about it. There is not one single, omnipotent source for all of the world's fortune cookies. There are dozens—if not hundreds—of bakeries catering to our cravings for clairvoyant confections. In their efforts to distinguish themselves in the crowded marketplace of prescient patisseries, these cookie bakers have diversified and specialized. In addition to traditional fortune cookies, you can get religious fortune cookies, humorous fortune cookies, rude fortune cookies, or even pornographic fortune cookies. Do you really want your future to depend on your restaurateur's vendor of cookies?

What's more, it's not only a questios of *where* you eat, but *when* you eat and with *whom*. Maybe you're running behind schedule and the waiter takes *your* fortune cookie to the table that was seated before you arrived—or to the group that came in behind you. Perhaps your dinner companion finishes his meal before you do, and then—without waiting—*he* hungrily snatches the fortune that fate had intended for *you*. How do you know when you crack open your cookie that what's inside will come true?

This may all seem a little silly, but the point I'm trying to make is that our future depends on all of the *wheres*, *whens*, *whats*, *whys*, and *whos* of our existence. It is always a question of contingencies, events that *may* occur. Possibilities.

Life is filled with possibilities, and even today's sweetest dessert is not a promise for a happier tomorrow. We never really know what the future feast is going to bring.

America's great poet Walt Whitman put it much better in his poem *"Me Imperturbe."*

> Me imperturbe, standing at ease in Nature,
> Master of all or mistress of all, aplomb in the midst of
>   irrational things,
> Imbued as they, passive, receptive, silent as they,
> Finding my occupation, poverty, notoriety, foibles,
>   crimes,
> less important than I thought, . . .
> . . . Me wherever my life is lived, O to be self-balanced
>   for contingencies,
> To confront night, storms, hunger, ridicule, accidents,
>   rebuffs,
> as the trees and animals do.

Oh, to be self-balanced for contingencies!

How can we find this self-balance? How do we remain self-confident and assured as we confront life's seemingly irrational buffet of contingencies?

Walt's answer is in the word *imbued*. It means inspired, permeated, invaded. So what does it mean to be inspired, permeated, and invaded? Let's look at them one at a time.

Inspired. What inspired our beginnings? What divine influence drew our parents together? Why ask the question: "Who would *I* be if *they* had never met?" We had no control over that inspiration; we were passive.

Permeated. What has permeated our lives? What spreads and flows throughout our days? Can we control and direct this flood of contingencies? No, we cannot. We can only be receptive.

Invaded. What has invaded our thinking? What enters our mind to confound our understanding? What do we say when we cannot find the answers? We say nothing. We remain silent.

When we are imbued as they—passive, receptive, and silent—then we are self-balanced for contingencies.

The future rarely proclaims "I'm coming." The future never declares "I'm here." The future arrives in all its irrational and chaotic splendor and it often renders our occupation, poverty, notoriety, foibles, crimes, less important than we thought. There's nothing we can do about that.

That's just the way the cookie crumbles.

Trusting the God of Potluck

THERE'S NO BETTER TIME to consider the importance of a balanced diet than on that perfectly symmetrical day we call the Equinox.

There are only two days each year that are equal parts day and night—light and dark—sun and shadow. In March this day marks the beginning of spring; in September it signals the onset of autumn. On either day, it's a good time to recall the lessons of equilibrium, and there is no greater teacher of balance than the God of Potluck.

I learned to trust the God of Potluck at an early age and to marvel at his mysterious ways. The insights I share with you now are gleaned from a lifetime of community suppers and 4-H Club picnics.

When the word goes out that there's going to be a Potluck Feast, there is never any doubt that (1) there will be more than enough food to go around; (2) the potluck will provide a perfectly balanced menu of salads, vegetables, potatoes, meats, and desserts.

No one plans it. No one is *in charge*. The feast is entrusted to the God of Potluck, and here's my theory on why it works so well.

It's all a matter of equilibrium.

First: A successful potluck is made up of equal parts of *competition* and *cooperation*.

For many, a community supper is the opportunity to

51

show off the very best their kitchen has to offer. Nothing is so gratifying as to be praised for your potato salad or to be deified for a splendid dessert. Others crowd around and ask for the recipe, demanding to know your secret, but you smile modestly and say, "I got if off the back of the box." Everyone knows there's more to it than that, but they concede that you have won. Without further discussion, it is tacitly assumed that no one else brings potato salad from now on. The others will henceforth fix their sights on perfecting casseroles, Jell-O salads, and dinner rolls. Over the years, the feast just gets better and better. Competition and cooperation. Congratulations and concession. Each in equal parts.

Second (and much more difficult): A potluck demands an equal balance of *compassion* and *contempt*.

Not everyone is up to the challenge of a highly competitive bake off. Often, these people bring that "mystery dish" that remains untouched until the plates are cleared away. Or perhaps they're the ones who never bring anything more than a bag of potato chips to the feast. "Not even a little dip to go with it," Aunt Flo would sniff. It's easy to feel contempt for the less than savory or for the downright lazy. There are a few at every potluck meal. But you must strive to balance that contempt with compassion.

As you sample the buffet at the Feast of Existence, it's fine to be selective in your choices. You prefer Mabel Hakey's baked beans, Aunt Opal's macaroni salad, and Mr. Soderquist's onion-topped dinner rolls. You always demonstrate particular loyalty to your mother's acclaimed casserole, and you sometimes take more than a generous portion of your own offering. You know how disheartening it is to take home a dish that has been barely touched.

Then, as you near the mystery dish, you turn up your nose and ask, "What is *that*?"—you take a sniff and laughingly declare, "It smells like horse meat." But your best friend says, "My mom made that." Then, with the same allegiance *you* had shown *your* mother, your pal plops a heaping spoonful of the brown stuff onto his plate. You do the same. You take some and you say, "This ain't bad." It's what you do for a friend. Equal parts compassion and contempt.

Third: At the Potluck Feast of Existence, everyone is respected as a friend.

We all bring our gifts to the table. Some of us become rich and famous for what we do, while others are less than stellar in our achievements. Some care enough to bring our very best, while others seem not to care at all. But at the Feast of Existence, we must never turn up our nose and sneer at others or what they have to offer. Take a portion—a tiny one if you wish—but try it. Listen to the story, look into the eyes. Don't send anyone away with her gift unshared. After all, it's what you would do for a friend.

Those are the life lessons of potluck.

Word goes out that there's going to be a feast, and you never know who or what you're going to find when you get there. If that feast is served and shared with respect—with equal parts competition and cooperation, compassion and contempt, cake and cauliflower stew, then the God of Potluck will provide us all with a balanced diet of infinite variety.

Trust it.

NEXT!

I'M AFRAID *the word* for the future is going to be *NEXT!*

With this single word we give voice to our greatest expectations, and at the same time we betray our most dreaded fears.

NEXT! shouts of our impatience with time, with place, with people and events.

NEXT! freezes us in a state of frustration.

NEXT! means always to anticipate—but never participate.

NEXT! leaves us forever hungry at the Feast of Existence.

There's a lot of pushing and shoving in the world of *NEXT!* As we impatiently wait to step up to the feast, we want to shunt aside those who stand before us, and we're equally annoyed with the people behind. We desperately defend our place in line, craning our necks to see what lies ahead, insisting that others "hurry up," but, at the same time, we're looking over our shoulders and selfishly chiding the next guy to "wait your turn." We're always waiting to get there, but we're never quite comfortable when we arrive. Between "I'm next!" and "Who's next?" there isn't much time to enjoy what we eat.

Consequently, in the world of *NEXT!* we can never get enough. With each new course we're asking, "What's next? What's new?" We barely swallow the first bite before we're gulping the next. Beside us sits the finicky eater. For him it's not a feast at all—it's a pill that must be swallowed. Our appetites could not be more different, but our question remains the same: "What's next?" We both leave the table hungry, because to be in the world of *NEXT!* is to be *nowhere* at all. It's only—and always—*NEXT!*

It's time to stop being *nowhere*. It's time to break rank, to step out of line, and to be *Now Here* instead—in the *here* and *now*. It's time to stop being so nervously *NEXT!* and to start being happily and hopefully *NEXT TO*—next to our neighbors, our family, and our friends. It's time to stop marching in single file like lemmings into the sea, and to start standing side by side on the shore.

What does it mean to stand on the shore?

Do you remember the scene in the *Wizard of Oz* when the scarecrow is wishing for a brain? He talks about all the things he could do, how smart he would be, the problems he would solve. One of his lines is, "Oh, I could tell you why the ocean's near the shore."

Why *is* the ocean near the shore? What and where is the shore?

To stand on the shore is to stand neither on land nor in the ocean; you're neither here nor there; you're neither this nor that. You might say that to stand on the shore is to be truly nowhere at all, but I think you'd be wrong. To stand on the shore is to be everywhere at once.

The shore is one of those mysterious ever-changing places of possibility and becoming. Just as rainbows are neither sunshine nor rain, and shadows are neither substance nor light, the shore is far greater than the sum of its parts. To stand in such a place is to trust in the reliable rhythms of living and to celebrate life's inevitable changes. We watch as the waves of the future roll in, and we mark the time with the ebb and the flow of the tides. No amount of impatient foot tapping will hurry the waves. No greedy gobbling will hold the high tide forever. We understand the futility of "I'm next!"—and we take delight in those we are next *to*.

To stand on the shore is to know that the friends to our left and the strangers to our right represent neither a throttle nor a threat on our journey to the feast. We're all there together. Today isn't the next and last train into the future. There's no need to push and shove on the station platform. There's no reason to fight for a seat.

The future will come to us as inevitably as the tides. We just need to stand next to one another on the shore and watch.

APRIL

The Perfect Host

*"The hope of the world
lies in what one demands,
not of others,
but of oneself."*

—JAMES BALDWIN

If You Want to Make God Laugh, Make Plans

THE QUOTATION BOOKS are filled with predictions about the perils of planning. The most famous—and ironic—is the one from Robert Burns. What that great Scot poet actually wrote was: "The best laid schemes o' mice an' men Gang aft a-gley." Sure enough, his poetry veered toward the vernacular, and we now quote him as saying: "The best laid plans of mice and men often go astray." Burns apparently knew what he was talking about.

My favorite maxim on the subject of planning is the old Jewish saying: "If you want to make God laugh, make plans." I like the notion that we give God a good laugh now and then. If all it takes to get a divine guffaw is for us to do a little planning, then we poor muddling mortals must keep God and all the angels in heaven rolling in the celestial aisles. No matter how "aft" our "schemes gang a-gley," we just keep on planning.

Now, I don't want to suggest that God is laughing *at* us. That would leave us to believe that God is a prankster who rains on parades solely for the purpose of watching us scramble for cover. God isn't a sadist. No, God laughs *with* us—which means, of course, that we must be willing to laugh along with God, to be a holy fool.

The Feast of Existence is best enjoyed by fools, but playing the fool is not the popular role it once was. Few of

us are willing to run the risk of looking ridiculous, and no
one wants to take the fall or to get a pie in the face. In days
gone by, however, the fool was an integral and honored
guest at the feast. All the best castles had one.

To play the fool meant having the opportunity—the
license—to open oneself to all that life had to offer. The
fool was permitted to try on all of the hats—even the
crown—and to take a walk, a strut, and a pratfall in everyone's shoes. The pious were mimicked, the pompous were
mocked, and even as the king himself was made a subject
for the fool's jokes, everyone laughed together at the folly
of their common human fallibility. No one laughed more
loudly than the king did. As a good host, he knew that a
good feast needed more than just food; it needed some
good laughs, too.

So like I said, God isn't laughing *at* us, but *with* us—
because God knows what it's like when even the *best* of the
best-laid plans go astray.

Imagine if *you* had planned something as spectacular as
the Feast of Existence. You thought of everything. It was all
there. All the bounty, the beauty, all the beasts and birds
and butterflies. You planned everything to be absolutely
perfect for your guests; but when they arrived they looked
around and asked, "What—no apples?" That had to be the
moment God said, "Let there be fools."

Since that day, we've been left in charge of planning the
menu ourselves. Just when we think we've got it all right,
something—or someone—comes along to show us where
we've gone wrong. Those are the times when it's most
important to play the fool and to remember that a good
laugh is as nourishing as a good meal—and more liberat-

ing. Each time we take a fall, we learn something new, and we bounce back up, more resilient and ready for the next round.

Good fools never give up and never give in. We just keep on trying, and keep on planning, and if through it all we can keep on laughing, then we can take comfort in knowing that God is laughing with us.

It's an Open House

ONE OF MY FAVORITE childhood stories tells the tale of a peasant, his wife, and their tiny cottage. The place was simply too small. They never had guests because there was no room at the table. They couldn't raise a family because there was no place for children to sleep. There was barely room for the two of them in that house, and they were starting to get in each other's way and on each other's nerves. They needed a bigger house.

Well, as luck—and fairy tales—would have it, a wizard arrived to grant their desires.

"You shall have a bigger house," he said, "but first you must do as I tell you."

The couple agreed to the deal and eagerly awaited the wizard's demands.

"First," he instructed, "you must bring all your chickens, ducks, geese, and fowl into the house with you." The couple happily brought in the birds. "Next," he declared, "bring in the dogs," and they did, "and the cats," and they did, "and the pigs and the cows and the horses and the goat." Well, the peasant and his wife pushed, and they shoved, and they squeezed them all tight—and still the wizard demanded they do more.

"Now," he proclaimed, "invite all your neighbors—and all of their animals, too. Put on a feast for them, and by tonight you shall have your big house."

It didn't seem possible that the entire neighborhood could fit into the overstuffed cottage, but the invitations were sent and soon the banquet had begun. It was a noisy and crowded affair, but a festive one. Eventually, every neighbor, beast, fish, and fowl had been welcomed, wined, and dined. When all had finished and bade their farewells, the peasant and his wife collapsed in happy exhaustion and put up their feet to rest. It was then that they noticed how spacious their home had become. There was actually room to stretch out and relax. The wizard had granted their wish. That night they decided to start a family.

The Feast of Existence is a lot like that story. It's an Open House to which everyone is invited and you never know for sure who—or how many—will eventually show up to eat. Like the peasant and his wife, the more people you welcome into your life, the more you will celebrate. That's the magic of hospitality. After all, it's the people who make the party!

"But, how," you might ask, "can you plan for such an event?"

You can't. You don't even try. And here, I'm going to turn to the New Testament of the Bible for our lesson.

Do you remember the story of Jesus feeding the multitudes? In all four gospels the same story is told. It seems everywhere Jesus went he was attracting big crowds of people. On one such day, the gathering was particularly large and no one had brought anything to eat. So, when the mob turned hungry, Jesus took five loaves of bread and two fishes, blessed them, and fed all five thousand people. There were even twelve baskets of leftovers to gather when everyone was finished. All four gospels agree on these numbers. All four agree that it was a miracle. All four tell the story.

Only *two* of the gospel writers, Matthew and Mark, report on the *second* such event. This time, Jesus had *seven* loaves of bread (instead of five) and a *few* fishes (I'm assuming a few is more than two) and with these more ample provisions he fed only *four* thousand people, and had only *seven* baskets of leftovers.

So, what have we learned?

1. You can never really plan for these things. Sometimes five loaves and two fishes are enough for five thousand—and sometimes you'll need seven loaves and a few fishes for only four thousand. And don't count on leftovers. You just never know.

2. The first time you perform a miracle of hospitality, everyone is going to talk about it—just like all four gospel writers reported on the first feast. But the next time you make your magic, maybe only about half the people will notice. This didn't discourage Jesus, and it shouldn't discourage you.

At the Open House of life you must learn to be accommodating, flexible, and resilient. People come into your life unexpectedly, and just as unexpectedly they sometimes go. The trick is to welcome them and to enjoy their company while they are here. There's always room for one more at the table, there's always a place for another child to sleep, and with a loaf, a fish, and a prayer you can sometimes work miracles. But don't count on it.

Getting Stuck with the Check

IT'S TIME TO TALK about who is responsible for picking up the tab at this feast. That's right, even at the Feast of Existence there's no such thing as a free lunch. Painful as it sometimes seems, we eventually have to divide up the bill and decide who's going to pay for what.

It's tax time.

I always thought the government should've flown the women of my mother's family to Washington to rewrite the tax laws. They seemed to have an inherent understanding about what was fair in these matters. There were five of them: my mother, her two sisters, their mother—my grandmother, and my grandmother's sister—my great aunt Florence.

Six times a year, these women, along with the children, would go to lunch in celebration of someone's birthday. When the time came to settle the check, one of them would take pen to paper and determine everyone's share using a most equitable code of laws.

First, whoever was celebrating her birthday did not have to pay for her own meal. However, the cost of that meal was not divided equally among the remaining four women. It had been determined that my grandmother (who was living on a fixed income) had already paid more than her share over the years, so Grandma paid only for her own lunch—except when it was her birthday, of course. The remaining adults were then responsible for whatever they had eaten, right down to the penny. This was because Aunt Ida seldom wanted any dessert and Great Aunt Flo generally had an extra beverage. Each paid for what she ate.

The cost of the children's meals were then totaled and divided equally among all five women—even the Birthday Girl. These women felt very strongly that they were all responsible for the children. Although Aunt Ida brought four to the feast, and mother brought only two, Aunt Mabel (with none), Grandmother, and Great Aunt Flo did not mind chipping in for us cousins. They knew our mothers had to foot the bill for the other 359 lunches during the year.

Finally, the gratuity was calculated and was, in its entirety, paid by Flo. She had married very well. She also picked up the entire check for the sixth lunch each year when it was no one's birthday at all. It's just "My treat," said Flo.

It was that easy. Everyone paid for what she got, there was a personal deduction of one birthday lunch per year, special consideration was given to the elderly on a fixed income, the costs for rearing the next generation were shared equally, the workers were always well paid, and she who had more—gave more. As far as I know, everyone agreed that this system was both equitable and fair. It was used for nearly two decades without squabble or fuss.

The women of my mother's family thought it was decidedly vulgar to quibble over money at the table—or anywhere for that matter. The important thing was to celebrate and to enjoy one another's company. For that pleasure, each of them gladly paid her share of the tab and no one left grumbling that she had been stuck with the check.

It seems to me that these same basic principles could be used to determine the tax laws. We all enjoy certain services and protections that the government provides, so we should all pay for it. Everyone has an interest in the health, education, and welfare of our children, so everyone should chip in. There are some among us who need a break now and then, and there are some who could use a little help from the rest of us, so special considerations should be made.

And finally, in honor of Great Aunt Flo, if we've been blessed with more than we need, then I think we should sign our tax check with a smile and say, "It's my treat." We'd all feel a lot better if we did.

If You Can't Stand the Heat . . .

MUCH OF THE GREAT WISDOM of the world is stuck on the doors of America's refrigerators. There, amid the shopping lists, cartoons, and postcards from friends, are the maxims and platitudes that collectively make up a veritable Emily Post for behavior at the Feast of Existence.

It was from the door of my grandmother's Frigidaire that I learned: "God respects us when we work, but he loves us when we sing." Grandma apparently held this to be the gospel truth, for not only did this woman work, but she sang out loud as she labored. Whether in her garden, her kitchen, or at her foot-powered sewing machine, she made music. I am certain she earned God's full measure of regard, for she had my absolute devotion and love. Every meal and every moment in my grandmother's home was sweetened by the joy of her song.

Since then, I have been served—and have served myself—far too many meals that were salted by the sweat and tears of an unhappy cook. We all have a tendency to turn our labors into laments. We welcome our guests only to collapse in dramatic display of how monumentally tedious was the *labor of love* that brought such a feast to the table before us. We grant far too many favors that are soured by the lingering aftertaste of obligation and resentment. We cry over spilled milk and we flat out refuse to whistle while we work. I don't think even God can respect such a beleaguered and unhappy workforce.

73

What's worse, the complaining never stops. Long after the work is finished, we continue to moan and groan and carry on into the night.

I'm not suggesting that we can all be like my grandmother. Much of the work we do *is* tedious and frustrating and mind numbing. Some of the work we do requires too much attention and concentrated care for singing. But for every hour of *complaining* on the job, promise yourself that you'll also find some time for a song. Eventually, the work will get done. No matter how exhausting and tedious the day, when you sit down to the feast, be ready to sing.

Remember: "Tired muscles are best massaged by music."

I made that up and would be most honored if you would copy it down and tape it to your refrigerator door. Thank you.

MAY

Please Come to the Table

*"Plurality which is not reduced to unity
is confusion;
unity which does not depend on plurality
is tyranny."*

—Pascal

Please, Wait to Be Seated!

YOU WILL NOT FIND place cards at the Feast of Existence.

Sorry, but those thoughtful little cardboard tents that shelter us from confusion and ensure that we are camped beside a clever conversationalist can be used effectively only at dinner parties. There, a good and gracious host knows that it takes time and planning to make sure all her guests are comfortably and suitably matched. The success of the evening depends on such courtesy.

But when, in the face of life's random and chaotic feasting, someone tries to employ the same tactic in crowd control, watch out! If someone says to you, "Please, wait to be seated," or "We have a place for *you* right over here," those are fairly reliable warnings that the Feast of Existence is about to become a fascist existence.

You see, some people find life to be almost unbearably *random*—too messy, too chancy, and too difficult to control. And after all, what's wrong with a little order? Isn't life tidier when there's a place for everything and everyone stays in their place? Doesn't everyone feel safer with a comprehensible world order? I don't think so.

It's delusional to think we can impose a seating plan on the Feast of Existence. Do we really believe that (1) the perfect seating order can be determined; or (2) we know what criteria should be used in determining that order; or (3) once that order has been determined, there shall be no other orders before it—or after? Such a Utopia does not exist. And why? Because, there never will be an agreement about the final solution.

Some think seating should be determined by race or ethnic heritage; others want to use religion. A few prefer gender, while many think income, education, and intellect should be used to decide who sits where. Some people want to sit only with people who look and think just as they do, and others would prefer that people with common dietary preferences be allowed to dine separately. There are even some very well-intentioned people who believe that at least one representative from each category should be seated at every table. In the end, however, the planners can't agree.

The next thing you know, they have forsaken their place cards for placards, and they're out in the streets wielding new weapons—not in a fight against *chaos*—but in a battle to determine whose *order* is best.

In an essay titled *The Pursuit of the Ideal*, the twentieth-century British philosopher Isaiah Berlin wrote: "The search for perfection does seem to me a recipe for bloodshed. . . . To force people into the neat uniforms demanded by dogmatically believed-in schemes is almost always the road to inhumanity."

Berlin urges us to watch out for anyone who declares he has discovered the perfect world order. He warns us against following these "prophets with armies." He reminds us that our quest for *order* will eventually leave us with nothing but the excuse, "I was only *following* orders."

That's why there are no place cards at the Feast of Existence. They're futile in the face of change and upheaval, and they paralyze us in our efforts to make sense out of nonsense. For as baffling and as threatening as chaos might seem, at least there is *potential* in randomness. As long as we have the opportunity for *choice*, we have the option to *change* what we can, the freedom to meet the *challenges* as they come, and the hope that, if needed, there will always be another *chance* to get it right.

Choice, change, challenge, and chance. Those are the main courses being served at the Feast of Existence. It sounds perilous, I know, but if you keep your eyes, your mind, and your options open, you can enjoy a nourishing and balanced meal there. Again, Mr. Berlin says it better than I: "Of course social or political collisions will take place . . . they can, I believe, be minimized by *promoting and preserving an uneasy equilibrium,* which is constantly threatened and in constant need of repair."

Order vs. Chaos. Neither side is ever going to win.

On any given day, our place at the table is only a temporary arrangement. We shouldn't get too comfortable. There will be new choices, changes, challenges, and chances tomorrow.

I Call Dibs to Sitteth
on the Right Hand

REMEMBER WHEN NO ONE trusted anyone over the age of thirty? Remember when "the establishment" was the enemy? Remember when we thought we'd never grow up?

Well, *surprise!*

What happens when "thirty" is only a memory and becoming "the establishment" is the threatening reality? How do we avoid being adolescents forever and grow up to be adults instead?

What is it our parents know that we have yet to learn?

The answer: "You can't have everything that you want!"

It's a hard lesson to learn for a generation that was hailed as "the best and the brightest." We grew up thinking of ourselves only in superlatives; to expect—no, to demand—only the best, and to insist that we should always come first. Now, as the painful lessons of "share" and "wait your turn" are being taught, we tend to pout and sulk and sound a lot like Tommy Smothers when he whined, "Mom always liked you best!"

Everyone wants to be Mom's favorite, to be the best, to come first in line. Can you imagine how hard that is for Mom? She has to be wiser than Solomon as she tries to negotiate the squabbles of envious children.

Think about it. When the two women came before

Solomon, both claiming to be the mother of a single child, the wise king determined custody by threatening to cut the child in half. He knew the real mother would rather sacrifice herself than to see her child harmed, and he was right.

Now, imagine if two children, two siblings, came before the court—each pulling on a woman's arm and each wailing loudly, "She's *my* mommy! Make him let go! She's mine!" What, in all of his wisdom, would Solomon do then? If he drew his sword and threatened to cut the mother in half, I'm afraid her offspring would only urge him on: "Yes, go ahead. Divide her up—I want my share!"

I don't think Solomon had an answer for sibling rivalry.

Neither, does it seem, do we. People around the world are suffering terribly from a prolonged adolescence. We all want to be the best, to be the richest and most famous. We take more than we need, give less than we should, and through it all, we insist that we are the most favored.

Worst of all, we all believe that we "sitteth on the right hand" (if you know what I mean) and this claim of religious superiority—more than anything else—has left poor Mother Earth battered and stained with the blood of her warring children. We like to think we're as wise as Solomon, and maybe we are. But we're still not as wise as our mothers.

Mothers are the peacemakers who, by their example, teach us that compromise doesn't mean that we have failed. Mothers are the providers who, by their own sacrifice, show us that sharing doesn't mean we'll have less. And mothers are the judges, far wiser than Solomon, who cannot love one child more than the others but can still bless all children with a love of their own.

You see, Tommy Smothers was right, "Mom always

did like you best." And she liked *me* best, too. When we figure out how she did that, then we will be as wise as our mothers. Then we will know that *wherever* we are seated at the feast, we sitteth on the right hand of all things wise and wonderful.

We will have grown up!

Your Piece of the Pie

"THERE'S NO PLACE for you here," he said.

The *you* was collective. It was directed at a classroom of unruly and apathetic teenagers in the 1960s. The speaker was a wise and wonderful history teacher who, seeing our future too clearly, was doing his best to prepare us for the years ahead.

He warned us about the economic realities that would render our family farms obsolete. He predicted how the new city shopping malls would leave our small downtown abandoned and vacant. He talked about the end of community and about the mobile society, and while he saw many opportunities for us someplace else, he repeated, "There's no place for you here, so you better be prepared to go out and . . ." and this is where my memory fails me. He said either: "Go out and *make* a place for yourself," or "Go out and *find* a place for yourself." Either way, he got my attention. For me, his words carried no threat—only challenge and opportunity. I was ready to go.

There was much talk of Camelot in those idealistic days, and I saw the world as one big round table with a place for everyone. We could go anywhere—do anything—be anybody, if we would just put down our swords and celebrate together. One big table—one big world—with a slice of the pie for each of us.

The world doesn't seem so big anymore. The sun never

sets on commerce and communication, and the boundaries that once defined "home" have disappeared. The table is beginning to feel crowded, and the only pie that's being served is something quite bland and homogenous called McHumble. It's starting to feel as if "there's no place for you here!" Now, however, there is no place else to go, and all over the world we are seeing increased competition for a place at the feast.

It's happening everywhere; people are clamoring for their own particular piece of the pie. In the name of race, religion, language, or special interest, we are cutting the slices so thinly that the wedges which once nourished us are being honed into daggers instead. All around the table people are pulling out and wielding these weapons of divisiveness and discord in the oxymoronic battles we call "culture wars." We all seem to be insisting that "there's no place for *you* here!"

That's why I wish I could remember if my teacher said "*make* a place for yourself," or "*find* a place for yourself." It's an important distinction.

If we are to *make* a place, that would imply creating, building, and contributing to the growth of the pie. On the other hand, to *find* a place would seem to suggest that someone else has done the work and that we need only to pull up a chair, grab a piece, and start eating. Given the crowd at the table, I think our choices are clear.

The world is only so big and the resources for pie making are limited. It's always tempting, once we have found *our* place, to turn others away and to say, "There's no place for you here." But if the dream of Camelot is to stay alive, then the table must remain whole. We must turn our swords back into pie shares. We must learn new ways to replenish the feast, and to *make* a place—not only for ourselves, but also for others.

We must learn how to eat our pie—and share it, too.

That's not a threat—it's a challenge and an opportunity!

The Cheese Stands Alone

NOWHERE ARE the consequences of exclusion more keenly felt than while playing "The Farmer in the Dell." I used to call it "The Farmer Goes to Hell." I hated that game.

Do you remember it? It starts out with a circle of happy, hopeful, hand-holding children, all skipping around and singing together. Then, someone is chosen to be "It"—to be the farmer. The farmer becomes the focus of everyone's attention, because the farmer has been empowered to *pick*—as in "The Farmer *picks* a wife, the farmer picks a wife, heigh-ho the derry-o, the farmer picks a wife."

After the most popular *pickee* has joined the farmer as his wife, the picking continues. The wife picks a child—who in turn picks a nurse, who picks a dog, who picks a cat, and so on and so on and so on. The inside cluster of the chosen grows ever larger as the circle of *wanna-bes* is diminished. Eventually we get down to rats and mice. And then—finally—we're left with nothing but "the cheese." And the cheese stands alone. Everyone else (the "in crowd") keeps singing: "Heigh-ho the derry-o, the cheese stands alone."

I really, really, *really* hated that game.

I couldn't wait to grow up so I wouldn't have to play it anymore. I longed for the day when I wouldn't be forced to dance and skip around with a big desperate smile on my face that pleaded *Pick ME!* And it only got worse.

In junior high school the humiliation intensified when it came time to pick teams for basketball, or baseball, or volleyball, or football. It didn't matter what shape the ball was; I rarely was selected to be on anyone's team. It was worse than being the cheese.

And then came high school: dating, "in crowds," and "most likely to . . . yes, always be the cheese." Just once, I wanted to be "It"—to be the picker instead of the picked-on. To be included. To be on the inside.

I still haven't found a way to avoid popularity games, but I recently discovered something quite by accident while doodling: being "It" is nothing more than being "I" with a "t" to bear. It was such a revelation. Our need for acceptance and approval is a terrible cross we all bear. Every time we go deeper into debt to wear the latest fashion or to drive the biggest car, we're back to skipping around with that desperate "pick me" smile on our faces. We travel to the right vacation spots, eat at the trendy restaurants, buy the books we never read, and read the subtitles at movies we'd rather watch—all so we won't be left standing alone. Everybody is doing it!

Yet while everybody is doing it, nobody really is "It." That's right. We're all just a bunch of well-dressed cheeses, skipping around and wondering why nobody is picking us to be in the "in crowd." But there is no "in crowd"—there are only the buyers and sellers of "It." And here's the irony: While we're circling, and enviously eyeing what the sellers have, *we're* doing the picking. We're what keeps the game going.

And that makes it a different game altogether.

Now, all the cheeses stand together—and all around us

the promoters of "It" are skipping and dancing and smiling and pleading "Pick Me, Buy Me, Be Me!" Without "The Cheese," "It" can be nothing.

So, "Heigh-ho the derry-o!" The Big Cheese isn't alone after all.

Dining with an Empty Chair

WHEN WE WERE CHILDREN, my cousins and I would go to the local cemetery for our summer picnics. It was always so shady and quiet there. We would spread our blanket among the tombstones and feel neither terror nor taboo, for we knew every name in the place.

There, carved in stone, were four or five generations of all the families we knew in our small Iowa farm town. We knew their names; we knew many of their stories; and I think we also knew that someday our names would be there as well. No one stays at the feast forever.

I remember very clearly the day I realized there was a grave waiting for me.

Every Memorial Day, my mother and her sisters would go to the cemetery to "decorate" the graves of the many family members who were buried there. First, they would go to the greenhouse and fill the car with trays of potted plants. Then, at the cemetery, they would walk the long rows of graves—stopping to remember a neighbor or a childhood friend—until they eventually came to a grandparent, or a parent, or an uncle, or a child. There they would kneel, not in prayer, but in a labor of love—the act of decoration—the planting of a small petunia or geranium. Then they would move on.

I used to go with them on these days. I loved to hear their stories as they recalled the lives that were memorialized there. Often they cried, but just as often they would laugh. Most of their memories were good ones. They felt very comfortable there, and, consequently, so did I. It was a nice place for a picnic.

My cousins and I meant no disrespect on those summer afternoons. On the contrary, we were always very careful not to walk over a grave, and we sat down only on plots that were yet to be filled. It was then that I first began to wonder who might someday lie beneath our picnic. My parents, my siblings, my cousins, myself? Would I someday have a grave? Yes.

Grave is such a *grave* word. So serious, so somber—hardly a word to describe a picnic. And yet, the thought of having a grave is always very liberating for me. We have graves because of gravity. And because of gravity, the Earth can go spinning and spinning through time and space and we never fly off. There's no need to hold on with white-knuckled fear. We can just go along for the ride. "Look, Ma! No hands! I've got gravity." I've got a grave. Death is a fact of the feast— *the* fact that spurs us to celebrate life.

Birth—life—death. All should be met with a spirit of celebration.

We should stop with the "rage, rage, rage," and start to find new ways to go gently and graciously into the long good nights of our death. Wouldn't you prefer to look up from your deathbed and leave this Earth seeing the same kind of smiles that greeted you in your cradle when you first got here?

Like I said, no one stays at the feast forever. Nor, however, do they go very far away. As long as we remember and celebrate the lives of those who are gone, our feast is in no way diminished. We will not dine with an empty chair if we choose instead to have a picnic with our memories.

JUNE

Dinner Is Served

"Know Thyself
was written over the portal of
the antique world.
Over the portal of the new world,
Be Thyself
shall be written."
—OSCAR WILDE

Table for One

To BELIEVE THIS STORY you must first believe that once there was a time and a place where people had no mirrors. That's right, no mirrors, no reflections, and—you might think—no vanity.

And yet, there *was* one very vain young man. He needed no mirror to attest to his superiority. He just knew—or thought he knew—that he was the only "One-Two" in a land of "Two-Ones." Let me explain.

You and I—and everyone we know—are "Two-Ones." We have *two* eyes and *one* nose. Our hero, however—let's call him Cy—decided that since *he* saw only *one* thing at a time, *he* had only *one* eye. That was only logical. What's more, if he looked to the left with this solitary eye he saw a nose—and if he looked to the *right*, there was another nose as well. It was as plain as the noses on his face; Cy was a "One-Two"—*one* eye and *two* noses. He was the *only* "One-Two" in a world of "Two-Ones." This distinction set him apart, and explained why he saw the world so clearly while everyone else was a cock-eyed fool.

The names said it all; as a "One-Two," Cy was the only *forward*-looking, clear-eyed visionary in the village. The others, the "Two-Ones," were by design backward, cross-eyed, and duplicitous. The only thing that Cy and his neighbors had in common were their single mouths, but what they did with their mouths baffled Cy. He rarely talked to anyone and had little reason to smile or to laugh. Singing was out of the question, and kissing made people look foolish—especially when they were using all four eyes to gaze dumbly at each other. No, the only use for a mouth was to *eat* with it, and Cy loved to eat. That was his problem; as much as he disliked being around the "Two-Ones," he had to admit that they really knew how to put on a feast.

There was always much talking, smiling, laughing, singing (and even a little kissing) at these feasts, but primarily there was very good eating. Cy tried to stay away, but once the cooking began, the aromas were irresistible—especially if you had two noses. Plus, all of the "Two-Ones" wanted him to be there. They always invited him, and never once did anyone mention his status as the only "One-Two." Oh, maybe now and then someone would smile and wink at him, but Cy knew this was their way of saying, I wish I had only one eye, like you. Cy pitied them, but felt it was best if he kept his distance. Whenever he came to the feast, he always sat at a table for one. He could get more eating—and drinking—done if he wasn't using his mouth for laughing and singing. Cy drank a lot at his table for one.

One day after the feast, when Cy was staggering home, he decided to wash his face in the river. When he knelt beside the water and leaned forward, he could hardly believe his eye. Some stupid "Two-One" had fallen into the river and was now staring up through the water with a baffled look on his face. Exasperated by the simpleton's plight, Cy reached into the river to pull him free, but just as his hand entered the water, the dopey "Two-One" disap-

peared. Cy kept stumbling up and down the riverbank trying to save the guy, but every time he reached for him, the
"Two-One" swam away.

Fearing for the idiot's life, Cy rushed back to the feast
and told the others about the drowning man. To his disgust, they all just smiled and winked at one another and
asked Cy to describe the imperiled villager. As he did, their
smiles grew broader and one of them said, "I think it is
time." With no further concern for the fellow in the river,
the "Two-Ones" escorted Cy to the village's sacred house.

Once inside, they led Cy to the far end of the room
where the wall was completely covered by a velvet curtain.
Without a word, they raised the curtain, and there Cy saw
the young man he had tried to rescue from the river. Cy
was so happy to see that he was safe, and the smiling and
laughing young man was obviously glad to see Cy as well.
They ran to each other as if to embrace, but were surprised
to crash into the wall of glass that separated them. The
impact really hurt Cy's noses, and as he reached up to rub
one of them, he saw that the other guy was rubbing his
nose as well.

This made all the villagers laugh. When Cy turned
around to chastise them for their insensitivity, one wise old
"Two-One" stepped forward and said, "Today, you are no
longer a 'One-Two,' but one, too." Cy was generally
annoyed with religious double talk, but he listened as the
wise one revealed the secret of the mirror.

Cy could hardly believe his ears, but there was no
denying what his eye—*eyes* saw: He was not a "One-
Two," but a "Two-One," too. Confusing, but true. It was a
sobering but liberating moment for Cy. He first smiled,

then chuckled, then laughed right out loud in grateful relief that he would no longer have to go to the feast alone. He looked forward to singing and decided he would sign up for voice lessons.

And so it is with us all. When we're young, we're convinced there is no one else like us in the whole world. Then, we grow up and discover there are many faces at the feast, all different—and yet the same—and ours is just one among many; there to laugh and sing and kiss with the others. Suddenly, the world isn't such a lonely place after all. That's the big difference between being twelve (one two) and being twenty-one (two one).

Of course, some people never get past the age of twelve. They insist on their singular status forever and never join in the chorus. They think they're alone, but they need to realize something Margaret Mead once said, "Always remember that you are absolutely unique. Just like everyone else."

It explains everything.

Graduating from the Kiddie Table

As SOON AS I LEFT HOME and went to college, I stopped eating supper. I no longer partook of the humble and homely repast that marked the end of a laborer's day. No, when I left the farm, I left supper behind me. From that day forward, I *dined*. My evening meal became dinner.

Dinner meant cocktails and wine and cloth napkins. Dinner was candles and rows of forks and separate courses. I still remember the first time I was served a sorbet in order that I might "cleanse my palate before the entrée." Imagine, ice cream right in the middle of the meal! Oh yes, dinner was sophistication, and dinner was what I wanted to be.

Soon after I gave up supper, I also stopped going to the movies. I attended the cinema to view films—usually foreign ones. Whenever possible, I went to the thea*tre*—but never the thea*ter*. I learned the hard way that no matter how thrilling the first movement of a concerto might be, one must never applaud until the entire work is complete. After that, I found the best way to avoid embarrassment in the concert hall is to keep your program open with one finger on whichever movement is currently being played. If it's too dark to see your program, then remember there's generally a fast part, a slow part, and another fast part—applaud only after the second fast part. This usually works, except for those times when you don't feel like applauding—then it's appropriate to simply sit back and either look pensive or nod knowingly. "Knowing nods" also work on modern dance and in contemporary art galleries.

I knew I was sophisticated the day I stopped renting tuxedos and bought one instead. I assumed there would be no turning back after that. But, one night, decked out in black tie, I discovered that *really* sophisticated people eat *supper.* That's right, supper—usually after the films, the theatre, an art opening, or the opera. (Incidentally, you can applaud anytime you want during an opera.) What's more, these late suppers frequently consist of omelets and toast. So, I started eating supper again. But, I had to give up breakfast. Who needed scrambled eggs when you could have omelets? Thank God for brunch! It tides you over until it's time to "take tea" in the late afternoon.

If it's true that you are what you eat, then I had become brunch, tea, dinner, and a late-night supper—overfed and pretentious—but still very hungry. I wanted to be grown-up and sophisticated, but all I became was aloof and alien-ated. I bought a condo and gave generously to the Sierra Club, Public Radio, and the ACLU. I never carried a cam-era while in Europe, and declared any volume that appeared on a bestseller list to be a "McBook." I do admit that sometimes, but only when I couldn't sleep very well at night, I watched television—usually old *I Love Lucy* reruns. Now and then, I sneaked into fast-food restaurants, and there was a time when I was tempted to buy perma-nent press shirts—but no one ever found out. Only once did I mistake tomato aspic for Jell-O, and then I tried to excuse my choking surprise and disgust by explaining I was allergic to nightshades.

When I was a child, I couldn't wait to graduate from the kiddie table and to join the adults when my family gathered for holiday meals. I wanted to give up childish things. Then, when I was an adult, I wanted to graduate from my family supper and to join the sophisticates when they gathered to dine. I wanted to give up simple things.

It wasn't long after the aspic episode that I heard someone say, "Some people don't know the difference between taking a stand and striking a pose." We were at a dinner party, and I suddenly had a craving for meat loaf and mashed potatoes. I was starving for a good old-fashioned Iowa farm supper.

Virginia Woolf once wrote, "One of the signs of passing youth is the birth of a sense of fellowship with other human beings as we take our place among them."

I wish I had learned *that* in college. I wish I had learned that it doesn't matter what you call the feast, as long as you find fellowship with other human beings when you take your place among them. If I had learned *that*, then I really would have graduated from the kiddie table and wouldn't have missed twenty years of good movies and great suppers.

You live and learn.

We Ought to Plan Something

EVERY YEAR on the summer solstice, I think of Daisy Buchanan.

Daisy is F. Scott Fitzgerald's "beautiful little fool," who in the opening pages of *The Great Gatsby* asks: "Do you always watch for the longest day of the year and then miss it? I always watch for the longest day of the year and then miss it." To which the bored and haughty Jordan Baker replies—with a yawn—"We ought to plan something."

"All right," said Daisy. "What'll we plan? What do people plan?"

Poor, beautiful, inattentive Daisy. She keeps waiting and watching and wondering what she ought to be planning—and yet, she keeps missing it. To use today's vernacular, Daisy Buchanan is clueless! For just across the bay is one of the world's great planners—The Great Gatsby—and all of his plans are for her. Daisy doesn't need to plan anything; Gatsby has enough plans for both of them. She just doesn't know a good feast when she sees one.

You see, Daisy is a snob and Gatsby is not. That's the ocean that keeps them apart.

"I think everything's terrible anyhow," said Daisy— "And I know. I've been everywhere and seen everything and done everything."

Gatsby, on the other hand, has hope—he has a dream— "his incorruptible dream." He's convinced that if he throws a party that is big enough, loud enough, and grand enough, that all of the world will come, including—and most especially—Daisy. His feast is one of the all time great "Everyone's-Invited-Open-House-All-You-Can-Eat-Come-as-You-Are-No-Holds-Barred" bashes. And the entire world does come, and everyone loves the party—except Daisy. "She saw something awful in the very simplicity she failed to understand. . . . In the very casualness of Gatsby's party there were romantic possibilities totally absent from her world."

So, Daisy just keeps watching and waiting and wondering: "What more should we plan?" And Gatsby keeps planning and plotting and pleading: "What more can I do?" He's clueless, too—but at least he has a dream. Anyway, it doesn't work out in the end.

But that's what I think about on the longest day of the year. I keep trying to decide if it's better to be Daisy—or better to be Gatsby. To yawn or not to yawn. To party or not to party. To dream or not to dream.

Generally, I tend to favor Gatsby. I only wish he had lived long enough to throw another party—one where he doesn't stand around waiting for Daisy, but jumps in the fountain himself and starts having a good time. Of course, that isn't Gatsby's nature. He doesn't plan to have a good time, he plans in order to realize his expectations—and we've already talked about the dangers of expectations. So, I have to conclude that it's rather foolish and futile to be like Gatsby.

Daisy at least lives to talk about it. She probably talks to Cole Porter about it and gives him the inspiration for *It Was Just One of Those Things*. Daisy likes to appear sophisticated and carefree. In truth, she is only care*less*. Most of the people who come to Gatsby's parties don't care about Gatsby, or his plans, or his dreams. As Fitzgerald tells us, "They were careless people . . . they smashed up things and creatures and then retreated back into their money or their vast carelessness, . . . and let other people clean up the mess they had made." As tempting as that sometimes may seem, I don't want to be like Daisy either.

Even on the longest day of the year there's not enough time to figure this out. If you care too much, and make plans, and have great expectations, you're likely to get hurt. On the other hand, if you try to maintain some distance, and sit back and let the world spin as it will, you're going to miss a lot of good times. So we ought to plan something—but what?

I propose that we declare June 21 a national holiday. I think everyone should have the day off. Some of us could make plans to watch the sun *rise* on the longest day of the year—others could plan to watch it *set*. Some can host great picnics and parties—others can opt to sit alone on the porch and read. Eventually, over the years, people will start to honor certain traditional ways of observing "The Longest Day of the Year." Some will attend sporting events—others will stay in bed.

That's what the holiday is for—*choosing*. It will be called "National Choice Day." And since it's the longest day of the year, you can have as many choices as you can fit in between sunrise and sunset. You can even change your choice mid-day if you need to. If you want, you can even choose always to watch for the longest day of the year and then miss it; that's okay. The only thing you *must* do is to choose to do something—and even if you choose not to choose—well, that's your choice. You see, that's what makes "National Choice Day" so appealing—everyone observes it, even if they choose not to.

It's a day for honoring all the choices, for acknowledging all the chances, for accepting all the risks and the responsibilities and for watching and waiting and planning and hoping—and maybe even for missing.

It's your choice.

Save Room for Dessert

ABOUT MID-WAY through the Broadway musical *Man of La Mancha,* Don Quixote soliloquizes, "Take a deep breath of life and consider how it should be lived." He speaks of spiritual integrity, of justice, and of courtesy. And then, among his tenets of chivalrous behavior, he cautions: "Do not pursue pleasure, for thou may have the misfortune to overtake it."

I'm afraid that is exactly the misfortune that has befallen us. We have so doggedly and determinedly pursued pleasure, that not only have we overtaken it, but we have commodified, packaged, and cheapened it until it has become a nuisance.

Consider music. Think of how wonderful it must have once been to hear a choir sing, or to go to the concert hall for the symphony or the opera. Days, perhaps weeks or months, would have passed without music, and then you would be awash in the glory of Mozart or Beethoven. You would savor every note, every nuance of the music. You would leave the hall hungry for more, wishing you could indulge such a pleasure every day of your life.

And then came Mr. Marconi and Mr. Edison. Now, we can't escape music—in the car, in the grocery store, as we wait on hold on the telephone—it has become the noise we derisively call *Muzak.* Pleasure pursued—pleasure overtaken.

We've done the same with storytelling. From magical

109

nights around the campfires, then to theatre and the movies, we've now come to television with hundreds of channels filled with nothing but mind-numbing drivel and brain candy. And the telephone. People once endured for years without hearing the voice of a distant loved one. Now, we have machines that screen those voices lest the caller be "someone I'd rather not talk to right now." We have only begun to see how the Internet will further cheapen the quality of interpersonal communication.

We can travel anywhere, buy anything, visit Christmas shops 365 days a year, and if it once was better to light a candle than to curse the darkness, we now curse the bright lights that keep us from seeing the stars. We have pursued pleasure with such a fervor that when we are afforded the opportunity for yet another delight, we have nothing to say except that terribly smug and dismissive phrase: "Been there—done that."

We are glutted with pleasure. We have not left room for dessert.

Think of all the young people who now circle the globe before they reach the age of maturity. Think of all the vacation and retirement homes that are purchased before middle age. Think of all the trips, all the clothes, all the cars, and all the pleasures we pursue and discard in just one year. Think of how exhausted and jaded we are with all that we have. And where do we go for renewal? Back to the shopping mall for even more.

There are times we should excuse ourselves from the Feast of Existence. Now and then we should leave the table hungry for more.

The next time you think you want to go shopping, try

browsing your closet instead. Try a few things on—and then decide what you'd like to donate to the charitable thrift shop.

Turn off the car radio. Sing for yourself instead.

Turn off the television. Read a book—or better yet, write a letter. Few things are as therapeutic as letter writing. To use pen and paper in order to share your life with a distant friend is a thoughtful and restful way to end a hectic day.

Take a vow that you will not listen to Mozart's music until you can hear it performed live.

And should you have the pleasure of visiting Paris, or Rome, or Vienna, or even Topeka—leave one sight unseen, one neighborhood unexplored. Leave one place in your imagination—a place you can long to see.

Leave room for sweet dreams. Leave room for dessert.

JULY

Mind Your Manners

"The great secret, Eliza,
is not having bad manners or good manners
or any other particular sort of manners,
but having the same manner for all human souls:
in short, behaving as if you were in Heaven,
where there are no third-class carriages,
and one soul is as good as another."

—GEORGE BERNARD SHAW, *Pygmalion*

When in the Course
of Human Events

AMERICANS NEVER TIRE of declaring their independence. Ever since those first stirring words were penned in 1776, we have celebrated—and insisted upon—our freedoms, our self-sufficiency, our "can do" spirit, and our rugged individualism. We are free to be whomever we please, to have whatever we wish, to go wherever we want, and to do it whenever the fancy strikes. We are forever declaring our independence.

So why is it that over the decades—even as our freedoms have grown—our declarations of liberty have become so increasingly strident and harsh?

For example, in 1854, Henry David Thoreau gave us a most eloquent and liberating declaration when he wrote: "If a man does not keep pace with his companions, perhaps it is because he hears a different drummer. Let him step to the music that he hears, however measured or far away."

By 1926 we had "wits" like Dorothy Parker, who wrote:

Now I know the things I know,
And do the things I do;
and if you do not like me so,
To hell, my love, with you!

By the 1960s, we were all marching down a less-traveled road, convinced that those who had blazed the trail

115

before us could no longer be trusted, and all the time believing *I Did It My Way!*

Eventually, all this independence led us to the 1990s, when the rock star Madonna declared in *People* magazine: "I'm tough, I'm ambitious, and I know exactly what I want. If that makes me a bitch, OK."

What if Thomas Jefferson had written *that* to the British in 1776? We would now be known as the United *Bitches* of America. Maybe we are.

It's time to take another look at what we actually did declare those many years ago:

> When in the course of human events it becomes *necessary* for one people to dissolve the political *bonds* which connected them with another, and to assume among the powers of the earth the separate and equal station to which the laws of nature and of nature's god entitle them, a *decent respect to the opinions of mankind requires* that they should declare the causes which impel them to the separation [italics added].

It was *necessary* to dissolve the *bonds*. There was a reason—a need—for a declaration to be free from tyranny and oppression. That's where we were "in the course of human events." Though it was necessary to declare independence, we did not declare ourselves to be free from "a decent respect to the opinions of mankind." In others words, "We're tough, we're ambitious, and we know exactly what we want. But that does *not* mean we are going to behave like a bunch of bitches."

That's the difference between being free *from* something and being free *to do* something. As Elbert Hubbard wrote in 1914, "Independence is an achievement, not a bequest." It has taken decades of constant vigilance for people to achieve—and to protect—a world where they are free *from* what others believe *they* are free *to do*. Freedom from the enslavers. Freedom from the tyrants. Freedom from the oppressors.

Why is it that now, when we are free *from* so many things, we are so insistent upon being free *to do* whatever we please? Why have we lost all respect for the opinions of mankind? Where are we in the course of human events that it has become necessary for us to constantly declare our independence and assert our individuality? Why do we mistake freedom for an infantile desire to tell the world to "go to hell"?

I know it's probably heretical for anyone in my generation to say this, but I never liked the song "Me and Bobby McGee." To say, "Freedom's just another word for nothin' left to lose," seems dangerously shortsighted. When our freedom *to do* mocks all we have fought so hard to be free *from*, freedom seems to be the very thing we might lose. As we strive to be free from the opinions of mankind, it makes it easier for someone like Joseph Goebbels to come along and say: "It is the absolute right of the state to *supervise* the formation of public opinion."

As we celebrate our independence and revel in our rugged outspoken individualism, it might be wise to take a tip from Confucius: "Straightforwardness, without propriety, becomes rudeness."

A feast without manners is nothing more than eating with the dogs. Then, it becomes necessary in the course of the Feast of Existence to declare ourselves free from the bitches before they devour us.

Don't Talk with Your Mouth Full!

"MASTICATING" is such a nasty sounding word. "Chewing" is a little better—"chowing down" is much worse. Whatever you call it, nobody wants to watch it happen.

"Don't talk with your mouth full!" is the first table manner we all learn. It may also be the one we most consistently forget. In our eagerness to tell our stories, we often fail to clear our palate before we open our mouths. Consequently, whoever is sitting across the table has the misfortune to witness the mastication of a meal he himself is trying to enjoy. It's hard to take another bite of boiled beets after you've seen them thoroughly chewed and in their final moments before they are gulped down someone's gullet. The only choice is to look away before the Salisbury steak meets a similar fate.

The same thing frequently happens at the Feast of Existence. We get together with friends and family, business associates, or neighbors. There is much in common to enjoy, many stories to share, and perhaps some concerns to express. As we sit down to our common feast of experience, we look forward to good conversation with good friends. And then someone starts to talk with his mouth full—and not always is it filled with food. A mouth filled with gossip, or rumor, or sneering innuendo is as repellent as a mouthful of battered beets.

It's always disheartening and disappointing to hear

someone speak unkindly of a mutual acquaintance. You had always thought you were all good friends. But now, you cringe as you watch the character of that person being chewed and chomped and slimed. Do you defend your absent friend, or do you join right in? Do you sit and listen and run the risk of having a friend's character maligned, or do you say, "Please, don't talk with your mouth full." I'm afraid there are very few times when we behave so nobly. At best, we look away, try to change the subject, and hope no one else will be so mercilessly masticated.

As unpleasant as gossip can be, equally distasteful are strongly held and loudly voiced opinions. How often have you mentioned that you enjoyed a film or a book, only to have it denounced as "terrible" or "trashy" or "trivial"? Have you had your religion ridiculed, your politics pilloried, or heard your childhood heroes chewed up and spat out as "phonies"? If it hurts, someone talking with his mouth full probably said it.

Talking with your mouth full also includes bragging, telling long, involved, detailed stories about your last vacation to Europe, or monopolizing any conversation with anecdotes featuring children and the cute things that they do. (The same applies to pets.) Sharing the particulars of your health problems—especially aches, pains, and prescription drugs—is also talking with your mouth full. And any public discussion of private sexual matters is always in bad taste. Simply put, if you find too many sentences beginning with "I" or "we," you are probably talking with your mouth full.

Everyone likes to share stories from their lives, everyone has strongly held opinions and beliefs, and everyone likes a bit of gossip now and then. But when we see the people and the things we hold dear being chewed, chomped, and swallowed with great gobbling gusto, we tend to look the other way and to seek out different companions at the Feast of Existence.

The next time you find yourself dining on someone's reputation, snacking on someone's feelings, or enjoying a steady diet of nothing except stories about yourself, remember you are talking with your mouth full.

Stop, close your mouth, and listen. It's the other person's turn.

Would You Do That at Home?

DO YOU REALIZE that you can change *guilt* to *quilt* just by turning around the tale on the "g"? Neat, huh? I wish I could think of some profound or clever insight about this little bit of wordplay, but so far I haven't come up with a thing. The only word I associate with both "guilt" and "quilt" is "Grandma."

Grandma was the person who taught me my prayers. It was at her house that I learned to recite "Now I lay me down to sleep." I never thought it was a scary notion to say, "If I should die before I wake, I pray the Lord my soul to take." That's what I wanted to happen, and that's exactly what I assumed happened when Grandma died— the Lord took her soul to heaven. Her prayers had been answered. She would be happy forever.

Then, one summer afternoon, Mom, Dad, my sister, and I were out fixing fences on the farm in Iowa. We had taken a lunch break, and as we rested on the grass before going back to work, Mom looked up to the sky and said, "I betcha Grandma is looking down on us right now." I looked up, too. Mom was probably right; I had no reason to think differently. Later, I asked my older and wiser sister what she thought.

She agreed that it would be *possible* for Grandma to keep an eye on us, but since heaven was supposed to be a happy place, and since seeing everything we did would probably make Grandma *un*happy, she concluded that Grandma *wasn't* looking down on us right now. That made me feel much better. "But," my sister warned me, "you never really know for sure."

It wasn't that I was afraid of getting caught doing something bad. I didn't think Grandma was a tattletale who would shake her finger and say, "I'm gonna go tell God!" Grandma wasn't vindictive. No, my real fear was that I would make heaven an unhappy place for her. I didn't want her to be disappointed, so I tried as best I could to be good. But try as I might, I did plenty of things in my life that would have made even the angels weep. So, when I think of guilt, I think of Grandma—and I wonder if I've somehow spoiled another day in paradise. That's guilt.

But, I also think of Grandma when I think of "quilt." In fact, I sleep in a bed that is covered by a quilt that she made. Back in Iowa those quilts are often called comforters, and that's another word that makes me think of Grandma. So, here I'm tempted to say: "Every time I do something bad, Grandma just flips the tale of the 'g' around and turns my guilt into a quilt and comforts me with her love." But I don't think it's that easy. Guilt is guilt, and a quilt is a quilt. Each is a legacy from Grandma, and I treasure them both.

You see, I don't think guilt is such a bad thing; particularly the kind of guilt I'm talking about. I think children should feel rotten when they disappoint their parents and their grandparents. It's the best way to learn how to behave at the feast. You grow up knowing that the people who love you want you to be the best you can be. They teach you your manners, and they teach you your prayers, and they make quilts for you, and they comfort and protect you, and they do their utmost to create heaven on earth for you. When you behave badly, you've spoiled another day in that paradise and you should feel guilty. If you don't like feeling guilty, then improve your behavior. The choice is yours.

I treasure my legacy of guilt just as much as I treasure my quilt. I got them both from my home.

Did your teacher ever reprimand your bad behavior with the question "Would you do that at home?" She knew you had been taught how to behave at home, that there were boundaries you dared not transgress, and that those same standards of conduct were expected from you while in public. Teachers and parents were allies back then. They were the adults. They were what you wanted to be like when you grew up.

Sometimes I think we must be such a disappointment to them. We haven't managed to teach *our* children how to take off their baseball caps while eating a meal. We talk a lot about children's self-esteem, but we've taught them little regard for the simple standards of courtesy by which they might ensure mutual self-respect. No one believes in shame anymore. No one believes in guilt. It's too bad.

Interestingly, there *is* a renewed passion for *quilts*. There's lots of talk about "stitching together the pieces of our families and communities and our world." All over the nation, people are coming together to make quilts with a fervor that borders on the sacramental. Maybe I'm a skeptic, but I think it's just another hunger for comfort. We can pretend to be our grandmas, but all the quilting in the world isn't going to turn around the tale of that "g"—you can't cover up guilt with a quilt. Nor should we try.

We have to know that there is a difference between right and wrong, between good and bad, between polite and rude, and between quilts and guilt. We have to know the difference between comfort and comportment, and we have to value one as greatly as we value the other.

I think that's what Grandma prayed for the most.

No, Thank You

SOMETIMES LIFE SEEMS like the setup for a bad joke:

"Don Corleone, Nancy Reagan, Ado Annie (the comic relief character in the musical *Oklahoma*) and *you* all walk into the Feast. . . . The Don makes you "an offer you can't refuse"—Nancy keeps insisting "Just Say No"—And Ado Annie is singing "I *cain't* say no!"

So what's the punch line? What's the snappy comeback when you have the mobster, the moralist, and the moonstruck lover all talking at once, each trying to outshout the others, and all of them shouting at *you*? What do you say?

What do you say to the Godfather? What do you say to those people who keep tempting you with bowl after bowl of mouth-watering goodies, always insisting, "You should try it, you'll like it"? What do you say when you can't afford the timeshare in Aruba, or when you're simply not interested in meeting your neighbor's niece?

Or—what do you say to Nancy Reagan? Or to the enforcers of both the Moral Majority and the Politically Correct? What do *you* say when *they* keep saying no, and every now and then, you'd like to say yes? "Yes" to a little frivolity. "Yes" to self-indulgence. "Yes" to a hangover the next morning. What do you say?

But then, what do you say to Ado Annie? What do you say to friends who insist, "If it feels good, do it?" What do you say as you watch them self-destruct? What do you say when they want to take you with them?

Here's your punch line. You say, "No, thank you!"

You walk up to the mobster and you say, "No, thank you." Even if he's in disguise as your best friend, you have the right to say no. Learn to use it. "No, I don't have the time or the money to cruise the Adriatic. No, I'm not going to buy your used car. No, it's all very tempting, but I'm full—I've had enough. No, thank you."

You can use the same line on the moralist. "No, thank you! No, I don't believe you are the majority. No, I don't believe you are always correct. No, I don't think I have all the answers, but then neither do you. No, thank you."

And Ado Annie can *hear* no even if she *cain't say* it. "No, thank you! No, I'm not going with you. No, you can't have the loan. No, I'm sure it would be exciting, but I'm not willing to take the risk. No, thank you."

Maybe it's not such a joke, after all. When the mobster, the moralist, the moonstruck lover, and you—a mere mortal—walk into the feast, someone is going to slip up now and then. Once in a while a mortal will yield to temptation, make a stupid remark, tell a tasteless joke, overeat, drink too much, and generally make a fool of himself. He might get a few laughs when he does, but generally he'll regret it. Eventually he'll learn to say, "No, thank you."

It's not much of a punch line, but leave the laughs to the comics and opt for "some respect" instead.

Sending Regrets

WHEN I GRADUATED from college, I was certain I wanted to be a teacher. More than that, I felt I was *destined* to be a teacher. I was *called* to be a teacher.

For three years, I made a valiant attempt to teach high school English. I was best at making lesson plans, better at preparing lecture notes, good at compiling suggested summer reading lists, but just plain bad at teaching.

At the Feast of Existence, I had always loaded my plate with heaping helpings of great books. With my new BA degree in hand, I had little regard for anyone who did not share my tastes in literature. The first time a sophomore asked, "Why do we have to read this Emerson crap?" I nearly throttled him. Relations with the students continued to deteriorate until I was called to the office of the principal. He was a gentleman with great patience, but no tolerance for sarcasm. As it seemed I was generating more than my share of parental complaints, it was time for a talk.

He suggested I use some of my sick days to get away for a long weekend. I assured him that I was feeling fine, but he persisted. "You don't always have to be *physically* ill to stay away from school," he said. "There are days when we need to attend to our *mental* health as well." He smiled and added, "Especially when we are working with young people."

I took his advice and enjoyed a long weekend. In fact, I took many long weekends—too many. It finally became clear that my call to be a teacher had apparently been a wrong number. At the end of the school year, I tendered my resignation and went to work in the world of advertising. It felt like a tremendous defeat at the time. In a few months, however, I discovered how much I enjoyed advertising—how well it suited my temperament and my skills. After that, I never regretted my decision to leave teaching.

Regrets. You can absolutely bury yourself with them if you're not careful. That's why you should always *send* your regrets. Send them away and wait for the next invitation. That's what I've tried to do with every disappointment, defeat, and lost love I've had along the way.

I excuse myself from the feast for a few days, I send my regrets, and then I take a long weekend to tend to my mental health. It's okay to heal.

I urge you to do the same. Learn to send your regrets! If you need to say you are sorry, say it—then accept the forgiveness that is given. If you need to end a relationship or to recover from a lost love, then do it with honesty, compassion, and grace. If your dreams are dashed, close your eyes and pray for new visions.

At the same time, you must wait and watch for the next invitation. One will always come. The trouble is, you won't know you've received it if you're still mired in regrets and remorse. At the Feast of Existence, nobody should cry over spilled milk. That is, nobody should cry for very long. Send your regrets, wipe up the mess, and look forward to life's next course.

AUGUST

May I Be Excused?

*"Our language has wisely sensed
the two sides of man's being alone.
It has created the word
loneliness
to express the pain of being alone.
And it has created the word
solitude
to express the glory of being alone."*

—PAUL TILLICH

Go to Your Room!

MARK TWAIN once wrote: "Few things are harder to put up with than the annoyance of a good example." I agree.

When Mary Poppins declares that she is "Practically perfect in every way," I nearly gag. There's no amount of sugar that can make me swallow that. No one is without flaws. Therefore, it should come as no surprise when I admit that I sometimes behave very badly at the feast.

I tend to complain about half-empty glasses, I say rude things to telemarketers, and when the weather turns inclement I whine as if it rains only on *my* parade. (I always take bad weather very personally.) I've been known to sneer at tourists, to speak abruptly to restaurant workers, and when someone's child is misbehaving, I grimace, roll my eyes toward heaven, and make that "tsk" sound with my tongue and teeth to let the parents know how disgusted I am.

I'm not proud of any of this behavior, and I wouldn't blame you if you slammed this book shut in disgust and said, "He should practice what he preaches." But before you do, remember that no one—no matter how despicable the behavior—is without merit. You can always use him as a *bad* example.

So give me a break!

I mean it—literally: "Give me a break." Send me away from the feast and order me to "take a time-out." Put me

to bed without supper, and there—like Shakespeare's
Bolingbroke—I will have nothing to eat except "the bitter
bread of banishment." Give me a break. Please.

Knowing when to leave the feast is one of the hardest
lessons we have to learn as adults. We're no longer children, and we can't rely on parents (or anyone else) to send
us into exile when our bad behavior threatens to disrupt
the festivities and leave us humiliated. We're on our own
now, and no one is going to give us a break when we get
too tired and cranky to stay at the party. It's our responsibility to monitor our own behavior and to heed that inner
voice when it tells us to "go to your room."

If you translate "go to your room" into adult-speak,
you get things like: Take a break, go for a short walk—or a
long run—plan a vacation, take a vacation. If nothing else,
just count to ten. Whatever you do, go away before you say
or do something you're going to regret. You're bouncing
off the walls. You've had too much sugar—or caffeine—or
too much of your co-workers, your spouse, your children,
or your neighbors. It's time to ask, "May I be excused?"—
then make a gracious exit and hit the pavement running.
It's time to "go to your room."

What does it mean to "go to your room"? What—if
anything—can be gained from solitary confinement?

Once, after a very difficult customer had left our bookshop, a co-worker turned to me and said, "I feel sorry for
him. We had to be with him for only thirty minutes. He has
to be with himself twenty-four hours a day."

We all have to be with ourselves twenty-four hours a
day. As long as we behave well, we can also be with everyone else at the feast. But when it's time to "go to your

room," we go there alone—with ourselves. There, it's just you and your conscience—and it's time for a little chat.

For me, my soliloquies usually begin with that old routine of regret—"Woulda, coulda, shoulda: I wish I would've behaved differently. If only I could've seen it coming. What I should've said was . . ."

Sometimes, I put it all on paper. The physical act of writing—of taking the time to spell out each thought—slows the turmoil inside my head. It begins with just words—feelings, names, conflicts, and worries. Then, I start to articulate more precisely the exact nature of the problem; I write a few sentences—something like: "I want to strangle Betty." And sometimes I write it again and again and again. Then, I rip it up and throw it away. I would feel terrible if Betty saw those angry scribbles. But she won't. That's the beauty of going to my room; I don't have to regret what I do there. It's just me, my pen, and the paper. When the anger has passed, I can go back to the feast.

I have many favorite "rooms" to go to when I need to be alone. A long solitary hike in the woods generally renews my spirit and restores my equilibrium. If I'm in the city, I go to the museum; I love to be all by myself with hundreds of other people. Friends use their cars for "rooms" and take long drives. Some people read books, knit sweaters, or walk the dog. I suppose there are folks who actually go to their bedrooms and take naps. The important thing is to have a place where you *want* to go; a quiet place when the feast gets too loud.

When the parental voice inside my head tells me to "go to your room," it's usually a very bad boy who is being sent into exile. But once the temper tantrum has passed, my room is my place of rest and renewal. It is here that I do "practice what I preach."

I intend to keep on practicing until I get it right.

Brown Bagging It

"BROWN BAGGING IT" is what you have to do when you can't make it to the feast. Just like a skydiver who proudly declares, "I pack my own 'chute," you'd better be prepared to say, "I pack my own lunch!" It's a declaration of self-reliance—of knowing you can count on yourself as you leap into life with nothing but your brown bag of goodies to keep you from crashing to the ground.

Like a parachutist, it's best to travel light. An over-stuffed bag is nothing but baggage; it will only weigh you down. So keep it light. Keep it essential. You must know what you need to survive. You must know what energizes you, what sustains you, what gives you the courage to leap, what keeps you afloat, and what ultimately brings you safely back to Earth.

Metaphorically speaking, friends are the "food" we need for the journey. I think of friends as being the fruits and vegetables of my lunch. The ones with the thickest skins usually travel best; they're less likely to bruise or to be spoiled. I steer clear of anything that requires high maintenance, and I watch out if it comes with instructions or conditions like "Best if eaten before . . ." or "Surgeon General's Warning." I also tend to stick with the old stand-bys. Kiwis may be cute, fuzzy, and very trendy, but there's not much nutrition there.

Give me an apple, or a banana, a good orange, or a

ripe pear—something, someone I *know*. But always remember: Never try to eat all the way to the core. Let the seeds remain like secrets—safe inside their pods. Never disturb someone's basic sites of renewal and regeneration. If you do, you can't expect these people to be with you for the duration.

Always leave room in your bag for something sweet— for music, and games, and literature, and laughter. It can be something all your own, or something you like to share, but never forget those things that sweeten your days. Take along paper and pencil to keep a journal or to write a letter. Sing. Songs take up no room in your bag; they travel in your heart. Don't be afraid to dance, or to skip, or to run. Play. Think. Remember. Hope. Take and do whatever you need to renew your spirit.

The wilderness is not a barren place, so keep your eyes, mind, and bag open to the treasures you might find along the way. To be curious is essential for survival. Curiosity is, as John Locke says, "an appetite after knowledge," or as Samuel Johnson says, "the thirst of the soul." Either way, no brown bag is complete without it. Curiosity opens our eyes to the variety that is the spice of lunch.

Finally, take care of the bag itself. You get only one, so if you rip it, learn how to mend it—if you stain it, learn how to cleanse it. And don't be ashamed if it's getting all wrinkled and saggy; that is the proof of an intrepid traveler.

If anyone ever calls you an "old bag," simply say "thank you" and be on your way.

Sincerely Yours

WE ALL HAVE those days when we don't want to see—or to be around—anyone.

The feast is simply too much—too crowded, too noisy, too hectic. Like Greta, we "want to be alone!" But then, in our solitude, we hunger for companionship—for someone to listen. The feast may be too much, but we're not ready for a fast, either. We reach for the phone because we want to have someone to talk to, but we don't make the call because we don't want to listen to what that person might say. We don't want to go out, and we don't want to stay in. We don't know what to do.

There is, I've discovered, only one recipe that will satisfy this hunger to be all alone—but with somebody else. It is, as Lord Byron once wrote, "the only device for combining solitude with good company." It is letter writing.

Unlike a telephone call—which is often intrusive, untimely, and a chattering half hour of mere babble—a letter is a reflective, carefully considered, and lasting testament to your thoughts and to your regard for the recipient. You have the time to collect yourself, to organize what you want to say, to find the right words, and to express exactly what it is that's on your mind. You select which of life's episodes you wish to share, and you frame them in a way that might amuse or entertain your friend. There is a beginning—a greeting, a "Dear Friend"—that is rarely said over the phone. There is a middle—a discursive, perhaps even a rambling stream of thought that flows without interruption or question. And there is an end—a closing—a "Sincerely yours" or a "Best wishes" or a "Love"; a final thought before you sign your name. When you write a letter, you tell a story—*your* story—and you can be confident that there is someone who wants to hear it.

You never get a busy signal or an answering machine when you write a letter. You never have that uneasy feeling that someone might be screening your call—listening as you record your disappointment on tape—but opting not to pick up the phone to hear what you have to say. When you write a letter, it is an act of faith that there is a friend out there, a confirmation that you are never alone. A letter is always welcome. Not even e-mail or faxes (though decidedly much faster and more immediate) are as satisfying and rewarding as finding a letter in your mailbox—the stationery, the hand-addressed envelope. A tangible object was created only for you, it has traveled the miles to overcome time and space, and it is now in your hand. It is a letter from a friend.

That's the other great thing about letter writing—people (some of them, anyway) write back.

There are many different names for the letters we write in a lifetime. Sometimes we pen an "epistle"—a long, formal, literary composition that conveys the most sacred and profound sentiments we have to share. Other times, we sound a singular theme with just a quick "note." For romance and intrigue we may send a "missive" or a "billet-doux." When we're in a hurry, it's a "memo."

My favorite word for letter writing is *correspondence*.

To correspond is to exchange letters—to send *and* to receive them. To send a letter is to share all your dreams and adventures, and to confess all your doubts and disappointments. To receive a letter is to know that someone else can have "one of those days," too. To correspond is to find in ourselves—and to share with each other—the encouragement, the strength, the consolation, and the inspiration that will nourish and sustain us in ways that nothing else we find at the feast can do.

When all else fails, you've always got mail.

Is This Seat Taken?

HAVE YOU EVER considered how much courage it takes to ask that question? "Is this seat taken? Is there room here for me? Am I welcome to join you at the Feast of Existence?"

And have you ever considered how important it is to be careful about how you reply? "Yes, it is taken; I'm expecting a friend. No, there's no room, this table is full. Go find your own seat, your own friends, not mine." Or—"Please, have a seat; we can pull up a chair."

Remember, you always have a choice.

Everyone, at some time, has been a stranger in a strange place. Every child has had her first day of school. Everyone has had an appointment with a new physician. We have all moved into a strange cold town, and we've all had our turn at being new on the job. Each time, we're asking: "Is this seat taken? Is there room for me here?" Each time we are fearful as we wait for a reply.

Once, at a college reunion, a good friend was trying to explain what he experienced when he moved from the safe familiarity of rural Iowa to the somewhat cold and impersonal land of suburbia. "It's like trying to get a place on the ark," he joked. "Everybody is already paired off two-by-two, and when they find out you're a single sailor, it's either get a mate or get off and swim."

Few of us like to be confronted with another person's loneliness. Few of us have the courage to offer a seat or to pull up a chair. As we grow older, many of us find that our table at the feast is a place where we are comfortable only with our friends. A stranger takes time. A new friend is a risk. Another place at the table can sometimes throw the whole thing off balance. And, as my friend discovered in suburbia, where there's seldom room for *one* more, there is oddly room for *two*.

In the end, we all travel alone, but we all have a right to a place at the table. We all have a need to feel welcome when we get there.

Is there anyone in your world who is looking for a seat? Anyone new in the neighborhood or just starting at work? Is there anyone who once enjoyed the comfort of traveling with a mate, but who now finds himself all alone? And is there room at your table?

Don't wait until the newcomer asks, "Is this seat taken?" Be brave and say, "Please join us, pull up a chair." Whenever you see someone looking lonely, make it a practice to think of yourself as the proprietor of the bar in the old television sitcom *Cheers*—remember: "You like to go where everybody knows your name."

That can happen only if we have enough courage to introduce ourselves and enough compassion to learn some new names. When we do, we find that our table at the feast grows larger and larger with each new friend. There is always room for one more guest, and no one will need to ask, "Is this seat taken?"

September

They Serve Who Also Wait

*"There is as much dignity
in tilling a field as in
writing a poem."*

—Booker T. Washington

Just Justice

We should observe Labor Day by taking a pledge to stop using the word "just" in reference to the work people do.

In particular, I want to cite two personal, but very important, examples: To say "He's *just* a farmer," or "She's *just* a housewife," is not only hurtful and thoughtless, but it betrays our ignorance and threatens the viability of the feast itself.

My dad is a farmer. Mom is a housewife. Neither of them are "just" anything. Yes, they are people with work to do, and they are people who work hard to do it well, but we cannot demean that work by calling it "just" any-thing—or "only" or "merely" or "simply." How can we say, "He *only* feeds nations," or "She *merely* raises chil-dren," or "They *simply* survive from the soil of the Earth?" Imagine the feast without them.

Instead of saying, "He's only a farmer," try saying "He's the *only* farmer." Scary thought, isn't it? Yet each time we dismiss and diminish the work someone does, we discourage anyone else from doing that work in the future. All of the food we eat is now produced by less than three percent of the population; and that number is shrinking. You can't think of someone as "just a farmer" and still expect to pay low prices on fresh organic produce at the supermarket. You can't refer to someone as "just a plumber" and enjoy the convenience of hot and cold running water. Don't say "just a factory worker" unless you are willing to travel on foot—naked and without an umbrella. In short, as long as we need food, shelter, and clothing, no one is "only" anything.

Now, instead of saying, "She's *merely* a housewife," look up the word "merely" in the dictionary. It means "nothing else or more." How can you say that a woman who is mother, wife, nurse, cook, chauffeur, laundress, teacher, preacher, mind reader, decorator, administrator, psychiatrist, negotiator, and CEO is merely nothing else or more than a housewife? Housewives are the only remaining true Renaissance Men left. They are merely indispensable.

And finally, never say, "He's *simply* a mechanic," or "She's *simply* a secretary,"—or a teacher, or a store clerk, or a waiter, or a truck driver. No work is simple—no worker is a simpleton. There may be professions that are less adorned with the trappings of wealth and glamour, but all work is valuable and all workers must be valued.

Take the Labor Day pledge. Instead of saying anyone is "only" or "merely" or "simply," say instead that they are *truly* "just"—they are honorable and fair laborers. Say "He's *honorably* a farmer," or "She's *honorably* a housewife."

Remember, you and I are merely guests at the Feast of Existence, and we are forever in the debt of those who labor to make it happen.

"Hello, My Name Is . . ."

Is ANYONE comfortable with a self-adhesive declaration of "Hello, My Name Is . . ." stuck to his or her left lapel?

I'm not. Nothing leaves me feeling less like Dwight Currie than having "Hello, My Name Is Dwight Currie" stuck to my chest. There I am, in a room filled with strangers, and everyone is tagged and identified—supposedly for the purpose of enhanced communication, but I always feel targeted and labeled for the purposes of informed consumption.

I feel the same way when a waiter comes to the table and says, "Hello, my name is . . ." Does he really want me to know his name, or has the management required him to identify himself for the purposes of culpability? Is that why doctors, nurses, checkout clerks, and auto mechanics wear name tags? If so, shouldn't we require the same from lawyers, the clergy, and teachers?

I fear that someday soon we'll all be wearing name badges that come complete with bar-encoded details on family background, educational credentials, employment history, marital status, criminal records, market portfolio, and net worth. We'll all be equipped with laser scanning wands and we'll skip the small talk and simply download one another's pertinent personal data directly onto our electronic Rolodexes. No more greetings, no more introductions—just the relentless beeping of consumption.

Until that time, I prefer that "Hello, my name is . . ." be something that we share rather than something we wear; something we say rather than something we display. We are people—not products—and our names are the titles of our stories, not labels to be read, scanned, beeped, or deleted.

The next time you hear—or say—the words "Hello, my name is . . ." remember these three things:

1. Names are given to children at birth. The gift of a name comes with all the love and all the hope that new life inspires. Names have beginnings.

2. Between the time that a name is given and the moment you first hear it—or share it—the bearer of each name has lived a life. We have all loved and lost, laughed and cried, celebrated and mourned. Every name has a history.

3. All the hope and all the history of that name is now being introduced—shared. No matter how fleeting the association, two names—two beginnings and two histories—two stories are coming together. Names have futures.

Think of all the times you hear the words "Hello, my name is . . ."

Now, think of the choices you have in how you might respond.

Waiters, checkout clerks, postal workers, delivery people, construction crews, even telemarketers are people.

They have names, they have stories, and they have hopes for the future. They and their labor are worthy of our respect.

When you hear (or read) the words "Hello, my name is . . ." that is the time to listen and to remember that everyone is a guest at the Feast of Existence. We share in the labor, and we share in the harvest. We sit down together to tell our stories and our hopes, and we tell each other our names.

To know people's names is to acknowledge their humanity, to listen to their stories, and to share in their future.

This exchange is not to be taken lightly.

September Songs

THERE IS A TIME to go along with the flow, and there is a time for quibbling.

This is the time for quibbling—especially for quibbling about time.

We've come once again to an equinox—the autumnal equinox—and as they say, "The days grow short." So once again, it's time for talking about balance and equilibrium. Or would you say—it is time *to* talk about balance and equilibrium?

Time *to*—or time *for?*

That's right, I want to quibble about prepositions. I want to quibble about "to" and "for." You see, I don't know whether to go with Pete Seeger on this or to stick with Ecclesiastes.

When the popular folk singer freely lifted the lyrics for his 1960s ballad "Turn, Turn, Turn," from the Old Testament, he changed that preposition, and in doing so he changed the expectations of an entire generation.

From the King James Bible we get: "To every thing there is a season, and a time *to* every purpose under the heaven." Pete changed that to: "a time *for* every purpose under heaven." That's what I want to quibble about. Time "to" or time "for"?

I've always found the original biblical passage (and Pete's version of it) to be the perfect song for September.

To everything there is a season—
A time to be born, a time to die;
a time to plant, and a time to pluck up that which
*   is planted.*

It's so orderly, so reassuring—so balanced. It includes almost everything you have to do in life. A time to weep, and a time to laugh; a time to mourn, and a time to dance. To get, to lose. To keep, to cast away. To rend, to sew. To love, to hate. Equal parts of all things. A little of this, a little of that. Work and play. Day and night. Good and bad. Balance. Equilibrium.

So, what's my quibble?

It's about those damned prepositions! A time "to" or a time "for"?

Ecclesiastes may be balanced, but it's also maddeningly vague. It's all encompassing—everything is there, but it's not very specific. *When* is it time to laugh, and when is it time to mourn, and to dance, and to weep, and reap, and sow, and sew, and rend? When? Are there priorities? What needs to be done first? And how do we get everyone synchronized on these things? It's hard to dance when everyone around you is weeping. If everyone is speaking, who is keeping silent? The Bible doesn't give us a precise schedule for all of this.

So, we have to make it up as we go. We do our best to fit it all in. We want it all, and we want to do it all, so we schedule, we "pencil in," then we erase, and we reschedule. We hurry, we rush, we miss deadlines, we apologize, and we reschedule. We promise, we plan, we procrastinate, we poop out, and we reschedule. We weep, we mourn, we lose, we die, and we resched . . . oops! We're out of time!

What happened? Didn't the Bible tell us we would have time for everything?

No, Pete told us we would have time "for" everything. The Bible told us there is time "to" everything. There's a big difference.

If we think we should have time "for" everything, our time becomes just that—time for the tasks at hand. We must make time for planting, for reaping, for building, for all those jobs we need to get finished. That's fine; it's good to have a plan—for the things we can plan.

But, can we plan a time for weeping, for laughing, for mourning, and for dancing—and a time for dying? These are things we cannot schedule. Nor should we try. These are the things that we must have time *to* do.

Now, if we don't have time *for* everything, how can we have time *to* everything?

It's all about prepositions.

"For" is used when we're talking about the object, the purpose, or the specific intent. "For" is very particular.

"To," on the other hand, is used to indicate the infinitive—the infinite. "To" is very open and eternal, as time is infinite and eternal. There is time to every purpose under the heaven.

Life is time. Life consists of the mornings and nights, the days, the weeks, the months, and the years of our time on this planet. There is time to—there is life to every purpose under the heaven. Life is planting and reaping. Life is getting and losing, and weeping and laughing, and mourning and dancing, and loving and hating. Life isn't *for* any of this. Life just is all of this. Life is being born and dying. In between, there is time. There is life to experience it all—if we don't insist on making, taking, or scheduling time for it all. Life is to—not for.

So, I'm sorry, Pete, but I'm sticking with the original: "To every thing there is a season, and a time to every purpose under the heaven."

I trust that balance.

I only hope Pete was right when he sang, "I swear it's not too late."

I'll Wash—You Dry

I ALMOST BECAME a vegetarian for no other reason than I hate to scrub roasting pans. As much as I crave baked ham, dream of pot roast, or long for a juicy, stuffed turkey, I dread the mess that such sumptuous feasting leaves behind. I feel the same way about lasagna. I detest muffin pans with all those little pockets in them, and I don't even want to think about stir-fry. In fact, sometimes the whole feast seems like nothing more than a thin slice of pleasure sandwiched between two thick layers of labor: preparation and clean up. You can't have a feast without them.

The one inescapable truth at the Feast of Existence is "Mess Happens." Not only do you have to break a few eggs to make an omelet, you have to clean up the sticky pan you fried it in. Those are the rules, and if you dine at the feast it's important to remember these two things: (1) Don't bite off more than you can chew, and (2) Don't chew on more than you can clean up. We tend to forget number two.

No one wants to get stuck doing the dishes. We would prefer that someone else be responsible for the mess we leave behind. But the luxury of withdrawing to the parlor for brandy and cigars comes at a price that no one can afford to pay. You can walk away from a mess, try to ignore a mess, or even deny that there is a mess, but eventually you're up to your ankles in garbage and something has to be done.

My dad made his one and only visit to New York City in the late 1970s when, due to fiscal problems, the streets were strewn with garbage. He was disgusted. "Why don't they clean this up?" he asked. I tried to explain. I told him about the money problems, the high cost of labor, the sheer numbers involved. "Seven million people live in this city," I said. "When you have that many people, they're going to make a mess." He considered my explanation as we stood at the entrance to an enormous skyscraper. "How many people live and work in this building?" he asked. I shrugged. "If they all took turns sweeping the sidewalk," Dad figured, "I bet that each one of them would only have to do it about once every ten years."

I tried to envision the CEO of a major corporation sweeping the sidewalk in front of corporate headquarters— or any resident of Park Avenue bending over to pick up a gum wrapper. Then I looked at my father. As a farmer he managed to keep hundreds of acres of dirt clean. The barns that housed his cattle, chickens, and pigs were tidier than the sidewalks of New York. If *he* could do that, why couldn't seven million New Yorkers clean up their own mess? Why would they rather pay higher taxes than push a broom once every decade or so? I had no answer, but Dad did feel better after I told him about the laws governing dog poop.

Mess happens. You can't have a feast without it. You can't have a banquet with all the fixings if you aren't willing to do some of the fixing. If you want waterfront property, then you have to be willing to clean up after a flood and pay the price of hurricane insurance. Floods happen. If you want to ski on snow-covered mountains, then don't complain about snow-covered roads. Snow happens. If you want to flirt with infidelity and feast on a fling, then you better know how to mend a broken heart, save a shattered marriage, and rescue a shipwrecked family. Divorce happens. Mess happens. You have to be willing to clean up after yourself. It's inescapable.

Think of the great feasts of history. They all ended badly because the people in charge didn't want to do their own dishes. The Romans lost an empire and almost two thousand years later so did the British. Marie Antoinette liked to pretend she was a simple milkmaid, but in the end she lost her head over cleaning up a few dirty cake plates. And whenever anyone waxes nostalgic about the grace and elegance of the Old South, I look at the slavery that made it possible, and I wonder if we will ever clean up the mess left behind by all those belles and beaus. Sometimes the mess is just too great. The feast isn't worth it.

So, is a baked ham worth a greasy pan?

Or, is a disposable pan worth a landfill?

Can you keep the landfill out of your own backyard?

Or, can you transport your waste to someone else's backyard?

Is cheap energy worth nuclear waste?

Who's going to clean up that mess?

Are you willing to sweep the sidewalk every decade or so?

The Feast of Existence is not just a slice of fun; it's the whole sandwich—including the layers of work. You get a little of all of it with each bite, or you go without.

There's a story of a young man who enters a Zen monastery to escape the noise and mess of the outside world and to find peace and enlightenment therein. The first morning, he is so anxious to get started that he's quite disappointed to find that his sole task is to prepare his own breakfast. But, he does it without complaint, eats quickly, and then rushes back to the Zen master and asks, "What now? What do I do to find peace and enlightenment?" The Zen master replies, "Wash your bowl."

That's it. That's the secret to peace and enlightenment.

OCTOBER

Would You Like
a Doggy Bag?

*"For where your treasure is,
there will your heart be also."*

—JESUS

Putting Food By

THEY CALL IT "material culture," but it means "stuff."

That's what my niece told me. She's a graduate student in museum studies, and since she's currently focusing her considerable intellectual energies on the field of material culture, she should know. As a material culture specialist, she will someday curate and create those marvelous period rooms that are—for me—the highlight of any visit to a large museum.

According to my niece, a successful period room is more than a mute collection of historic furnishings. It is an exhibit of human artifacts—those treasures and trinkets that speak volumes about the people who once inhabited the room: who they were, how they lived, and what they valued most in life.

I wonder what artifacts the material culture specialists in the year 3000 will curate for the rooms of our time. What treasures, amid all the junk we leave behind, will someone's niece select to give voice to way we lived our lives? What will be preserved and displayed from our time at the feast?

Here are my suggestions:

People in the year 3000 should know that we had lots and lots and lots of *stuff*, so start with shelves, cupboards, cabinets, and closets—but keep them all shut. Museumgoers in the year 3000 don't need to know what we kept behind closed doors. They are, however, welcome to peruse those items we display on our shelves.

Books. I'd like future museumgoers to know that books were sacred to us. We had faith in learning and literature, and we proudly confessed that faith through the amassment and display of our books.

The *great* curator will have lots of bookmarks sticking out of the books. She will explain to museum visitors that these curious little pieces of paper were used to mark our favorite passages in the many, many books found on the shelves. Then, she will solemnly and carefully open a book to a marked passage and read it reverently to the people on the tour. They won't understand why the words were so special to us, but they will nod and sigh and long for the simpler time such a practice suggests.

What they won't know—and neither will the curator—is that the bookmark was left in the part of the book where the reader got so bored that she closed the volume and never came back to it. Sometime in the year 3025 that truth will be discovered, and it will spark great controversy in the world of museum studies. Material culture specialists will divide into two camps: those who continue to place books on the shelves and those who shove the books aside in order to make room for the television sets and rows and rows and rows of video tapes. What will that say about the inhabitants of these rooms?

Will curators know that this was the time when many people stopped participating and turned into spectators instead? Will they understand how the remote control turned one-time athletes into couch potatoes? How will the curator explain headsets? Will the period rooms include a piano? "Why," they will ponder, "are there record albums, cassette tapes, *and* CDs all of the same music?"

What the museumgoers will like best will be our photographs. The guides will tell them about cheap cameras and two-for-one film processing. The visitors will find it fascinating to see the same person standing in front of Big Ben, the Eiffel Tower, the Great Wall of China, the Sydney Opera House, the Pyramids, and the Statue of Liberty. "Didn't these people ever stay at home?" they will ask, and at this point the curator will open a closet and show them the T-shirts. The visitors will gasp, and then rush to the gift shop to buy a T-shirt of their own.

In an attempt to confound some material culture specialists of the future, I've created a little grouping of personal artifacts that defies explanation to anyone but me. It includes three items. The largest is a toy truck. Next to it, I have a photograph of me and that same truck that was taken on my third birthday; the truck was my gift. Now, any material culture specialist worth her advanced degree will be able to put those two together. But, what will she make of the third artifact, the recording of *My Fair Lady*? How long will it take—how much research will she have to do—before she discovers that Julie Andrews had her Broadway debut on the same day that I celebrated my third birthday and got that truck? How will she ever understand the significance of my personal little celebration of the feast?

We all celebrate the feast in our own way, and we all amass and preserve the unique treasure trove of trinkets that gives testament to how we live and what we hold dear. But in this, the most material of all material cultures, the trick is knowing what's treasure and what's trash.

Who's to say which is which?

This Isn't What I Ordered

SOME PEOPLE call it karma. Others like to say "What goes around, comes around." At the Feast of Existence we might call it "just desserts." But no matter how you say it, it comes to the same thing: "As ye sow, so shall ye reap." So universal is this belief that every major world religion adheres to some articulation of this truth.

Unfortunately, like so much of the received wisdom of the world, we have twisted this simple truth into a convenient catchall explanation for all the mysteries and miseries that defy our understanding and exceed our capacity for compassion. With it, we look at someone else's troubles and too quickly conclude, "He got what he deserved." Is he poor? He must be lazy. Is she sick? She must be sinful. We've turned this truth on its head to say, "As ye reap, so must have ye sown." We've put the harvest before the planting.

There are many times we are served a bitter dish at the Feast of Existence, but that does not mean we nurtured a crop of poison. It's difficult to imagine what seeds of anger a battered child may have sown that she should reap such abuse, or what seeds of pain the victims of torture and terrorism planted. If it were this simple, we would have to agree with the purveyors of fear and hatred who insist that survival is only for the fittest and that disease in an act of divine retribution.

We don't always get exactly what we ordered.

167

But life isn't only about what we *get,* it's also what we *give*—not what we reap, but what we sow. The joy is in the planting, because as any farmer will tell you, the harvest is never guaranteed. That's the truth about sowing and reaping. It's not a sure thing. You don't always get what you deserve. You don't always deserve what you get.

The feast will sometimes be greater—or less—than the harvest of your own individual sowing. You ultimately have no choice in that, but you do have the choice about how to behave. You owe it to yourself to opt for what brings you respect and loving admiration. That's the challenge of sowing and reaping.

Since our behavior at the feast can be nothing greater than the harvest of our own sowing, I think we should heed this teaching in all of its manifestations.

The Buddhist and the Christian variations read almost the same. In the first case you have: "It is nature's rule that as we sow, we shall reap." From the second you get: "Whatever a man sows, that he will also reap." In both cases it is important to note that the sowing comes first, and it follows that we should not expect to reap anything better than what we planted. Also note, however, that nothing is said about weeds, floods, drought, or locust. It simply says: "Plant a radish and you get a radish"—maybe—along with a lot of other things you didn't plant. This is where behavior becomes important.

As Confucius says: "What proceeds from you will return to you." In Judaism, the saying goes: "One who waters will himself be watered," and in Hinduism they say: "As thou dost plant the tree so it will grow." These maxims seem to suggest a more active role in the care of our garden. We don't simply sow and then sit back and wait to reap the harvest, we must also nurture and water and tend to what is best. And we must acknowledge and determine what to do about the weeds.

It's impossible to imagine a garden infested with more noxious and poisonous growth than that which grew in Nazi Germany. And yet, even in an evil place that was not of his own planting, Primo Levi remembered that "we must not become beasts; that even in this place one can survive . . . and that to survive we must force ourselves to save at least the skeleton, the scaffolding, the form of civilization. We are slaves, deprived of every right, exposed to every insult, condemned to certain death, but we still possess one power, and we must defend it with all our strength for it is the last—the power to refuse our consent."

It is true that we must reap the harvest we have sown. We must take responsibility for our own mistakes and misdeeds just as we take delight in our success and achievements. But we don't have to give our consent to everything that grows in the garden. We have choices. Some mushrooms are poisonous and some nightshades are deadly. It's important to know which is which, and not to blame the rose for the thistle that grows by her side.

It's not simply a question of sowing and reaping, but a lifetime of tending, nurturing, watering, and weeding. If it is true that "As we sow, so shall we reap," then I maintain that it's equally true that "As we garden, so shall we be esteemed."

Connoisseurs of Fine Whines

IT ALL BEGAN with *Queen for a Day*. Do you remember it? It was a television game show in the 1960s where women competed for prizes and a crown by telling the sad stories of their lives.

The show opened with each of three contestants detailing the miseries that qualified her for competition: financial ruin, sick children, errant husbands, injured pets, flood-ravaged homes. The hardships were real, the stories were sad, and the host was an expert at reducing the would-be queens to wracking sobs as they gasped and gulped and shared their woes. Then, there was a commercial break—after which we would return to find out who won.

The judging was quite simple. As each hopeful hopeless case recapped her miserable qualifications, the audience responded with an ovation that was measured by a needle on the "applause-o-meter" at the bottom of the screen. Whoever told the saddest story got the most applause, and she was crowned *Queen for a Day*. She also got a robe, some roses, and many wonderful prizes before she was led down the runway shedding tears of joy. The only thing missing was Bert Parks.

The other contestants received the aptly dubbed consolation prizes and were sent home with the understanding that either their lives weren't miserable enough to earn a crown, or they simply hadn't sobbed with great enough conviction. Either way, they lost—again. Then, the host smiled and invited us to "tune in again tomorrow" when three more woeful women would vie for the title of *Queen for a Day!* There was a parting shot of the current monarch of misery, then sign off and the roll of credits.

Please don't get me wrong. These women had real problems, they shed real tears, and it was gratifying to see their load lightened by a gift of cash and a few new appliances. Charity should not be mocked, but *competing* for charity is another matter.

I'm guessing most early viewers of *Queen for a Day* watched the program with sympathetic tears, then turned off their sets with a grateful sigh of, "There but for the grace of God go I." They sat down to count their blessings, grateful that they did not qualify as contestants. They had no desire to be victims. No one had to rescue them.

At the same time, the 1960s was also the decade that prompted millions of people to march in legitimate protest of some very real social and political ills. Racial discrimination, senseless war, and environmental devastation all had to be stopped. We linked arms, took to the streets, and made a difference—we won. We were crowned the "Best and the Brightest" and went on to win all the cash and prizes the 1980s had to offer. But unlike the viewers of *Queen for a Day, we* hungered for more.

If crying and protesting had won prizes in the past, then we'd simply have to find more wounds to weep about and more wrongs to right. No matter how idiosyncratic or *personal* the injustice, we did our best to qualify as victims in the competition for rewards. The result is what the social critic Robert Hughes has dubbed as the "Culture of Complaint." Put simply, whoever has the saddest story wins.

Again, I want to emphasize that I am not mocking legitimate complaints. It's an imperfect world, and there is much misery and injustice that cries out for our attention. I know that many people have a great deal to complain about. I just don't happen to be one of them—and neither are ninety percent of the rest of the population. So, what *am* I complaining about? Nothing; I simply want us to enjoy the feast. I want us to stop *competing* to be Queen for a Day.

During a recent case of influenza, I realized that I qualified as a victim for a vast number of reasons. I was once bullied on the playground, it is almost certain that I was discriminated against because I did not attend an Ivy League school, I'm slightly below average height, slightly above average weight, I pay more than my share of taxes, get less than my share of government handouts, and the chain-store book retailers are threatening to drive me out of business and destroy literature. What's more, my gender, age, race, and political affiliations are all potential reasons for complaint. If you spend two or three days watching daytime television talk shows, you, too, can be crowned a loser. I felt miserable. Happily, I recovered from the flu, went back to work, and found I had nothing to complain about at all.

I believe in work; I believe in charity; and I believe in political activism. But I don't believe that any of that qualifies me for coronation as the poster boy for self-sacrifice and misery. Give me an enthusiastic and joyous "Atta Boy!" any day over the patronizing and mawkish "Whatsa Matter?"

I'll compete to be a winner, but I'm not interested in being crowned a whiner.

The Crumbs That Fall from the Table

DO YOU REMEMBER "Trickle-Down Economics"? It was the popular theory of the 1980s that predicted a flood of wealth for the rich that would eventually "trickle down" to the poor. The aquatic metaphor was stretched even further when the wizards of Wall Street promised a rising tide of good fortune that would "lift everyone's boat." Unfortunately, not everyone had a boat, and the wealth at the top was less fluid than they thought. No matter how you looked at it, the poor were either going to dehydrate or drown.

Trickle-Down Economics was as heartless as saying "Let them eat cake." In fact, it was worse. It was more like saying "Let them eat the *crumbs* of the cake that fall from my table."

This is not acceptable behavior at the Feast of Existence!

"Leftover" is not a synonym for "charity."

Charity derives from the same Latin word as cherish, caress, and care. And *care* rhymes with *share*. So when you think of charity, you should think of what it means to care enough to share what you can spare of your cherished fare.

Leftover, on the other hand, has no etymological pedigree. It is a relatively new word in our language. It's a nicer way of saying scrap. And we won't go into what rhymes with scrap.

All over this world, in every country, in every state, city, and town, and in every neighborhood and family, there are people in need of our charity. People who need a caress—people who need our care. Can we, in good conscience, ask them to settle for the meager crumbs that fall from our table? Is it enough to say, "I pay my taxes, let the government take care of them"? Can't we care enough to share?

But, you say you have so little to spare? So little of what? Money?

Charity does not always have to mean money. In fact, many people say *time* is money, so perhaps you can give of your time. Not enough of that, either? Then start thinking creatively.

I once knew a woman who wanted to brush up her skills at the piano. She had neither the money to buy an instrument, nor did she have the time to devote to practice. Her solution was inspired. She went to a neighborhood church and got permission to use a piano during her lunch break. The next day when she arrived for her practice session, she found many senior citizens were at the church for their free noontime meal. This didn't stop my friend. She turned her practice into a performance, and ever since, the senior citizens of the parish enjoy classical music as they enjoy their feast.

Do you have a talent you can share?

Do you love to read? Then read for the blind—or make recordings for the public library. Maybe you could volunteer for storytime with the neighborhood children. Perhaps you should clear away some of your many books and donate them for a good cause.

Can you give an elderly neighbor a ride the next time you go to the grocery store?

Can you help your friend's son with his algebra homework?

Does the playground equipment need repair? Do the park benches need painting?

Do you care enough to share what you can spare?

This doesn't mean getting rid of your junk; it means taking the television out of the guest bedroom and giving it to someone who will watch it. It means opening your closet and removing some of those sweaters that could keep dozens of people warm. It means clipping coupons for the grocery store, then donating all the bargains you find to the local food pantry.

Charity means sharing. It means cutting your cake into as many slices as you can, and then inviting everyone to join you at the feast.

You'll be surprised how much better everything tastes.

Trick or Treat?

HALLOWEEN is another one of those holidays that needs to be reexamined. Instead of simply being an excuse for children to go begging as ghosts, ghouls, and television superheroes, Halloween should be observed as one of those pivotal times during the year when decisions have to be made concerning what to do next and how to proceed.

For Celtic cultures, Halloween marked the last day of the year and was observed in anticipation of All Saint's Day, which was celebrated the following morning. On this night before the festival, it was believed that the spirits of the dead roamed the countryside as they made their way back to their former homes. This meant that witches, demons, and goblins were also abroad, so when you heard the knock on the door, it was with genuine fear and trembling that you lifted the latch. You didn't know whether you'd be greeting the ghost of a departed loved one or welcoming an evil spirit into your home. But you had no choice. On Halloween you had to face your fears head-on. This was not the time to hide from the shadows.

It isn't simply by chance that Halloween appears on the calendar in exact opposition to Groundhog Day. Halloween, like Whitsunday (in May) and Lammas (in August), is a quarter day—the days that mark the mid-points between a solstice and an equinox. Another quarter day is February 2, which in this country we call Groundhog Day, but on the liturgical calendar it is known as Candlemas. Actually, Groundhog Day and Candlemas are basically concerned with the same thing—shedding a little light on winter in an attempt to hasten the spring. The point is, if Groundhog Day is the time to turn *away* from the shadows and to face the sun, then Halloween is the time to face the shadows head-on and to turn away from our *fears*.

Fears can paralyze us, and with only six more weeks before the onset of winter, this is not the time to be frozen in fear. We need all the courage we can muster to face the long days of darkness that lie ahead. During those dark days, we will come together for some of the really great feasting of the year. If we let our fears control us, we will miss the fun. If, when fear knocks, we cower behind locked doors, then we have only locked ourselves in. Fear is persistent. It will wait on your doorstep forever. It's best just to open the door and to let fear in.

And what are our fears?

In his great novel *Crime and Punishment,* Fyodor Dostoyevski wrote: "What people fear most is taking a new step." The fear of the unknown. The fear of failing. The fear that somehow you will lose yourself. These are the terrible fearful shadows that paralyze us with dread and trembling. But, if you face those fears and take that new step, you're going to learn something about shadows that makes them seem a little less frightening.

As you step forward and put your foot firmly on the ground, you will notice that your shadow begins where your foot touches the Earth. That shadow confirms your humanity. It marks your place on the Earth. It assures you that you haven't disappeared. That shadow is the dancing partner that follows *your* lead. So take another step toward the unknown—and now, it is known. Take another step toward your goal—and the success of that single step means you'll never really fail.

Shadows are the inescapable companions that are always with us at the feast. We need to acknowledge their presence and engage them in the dance.

Halloween is the perfect time of year to decide whether our shadows will *trick* us into paralysis, or *treat* us to new adventures.

NOVEMBER

We Gather Together

*"Continuity with the past
is not a duty,
only a necessity."*

—OLIVER WENDELL HOLMES

Give and Take

I REMEMBER the first time my mother told me, "It's better to give than to receive." It was after a 4-H Club holiday gift exchange when I got stuck with a lint brush. Her maxim did little to ease my disappointment. I thought, if it's better to give, then maybe it's *best* to receive. After all, it was at 4-H where I also learned:

> *Good, better, best*
> *Never let it rest—*
> *'Til your good is better*
> *And your better is best!*

But, I was wrong; it's not *best* to receive.
It is good to receive.
It is better to give.
But it's best to give *and* receive.
Or, to put it another way—it's best to "give and take"—to learn to compromise.

Compromise is one of those words that has taken on rather bad connotations these days. We hear people proudly declare that they "will not compromise their principles," or their values, or their standards. Fine. We all need principles, values, and standards. But to use the word compromise in this way is inaccurate.

The word "compromise" is one of the most beautiful

words in our language, for its real meaning is not to "cave in," but to "make a mutual promise."

A *mutual promise*—the very basis of civilized behavior. What is marriage if not a mutual promise? And business contracts, and the rules to play Bridge? Does anyone like to wait at stoplights? Wouldn't it be *good* if you could just speed through the city? But isn't it *better* that you don't? And isn't it *best* that all drivers have made a mutual promise to obey the laws?

Laws. Sometimes we have to clear away the feast and sit down at the table to make some tough decisions about how to behave. We have to "deliberate," which means to "intend to liberate," which comes from the Latin word *libra*—the scales. To deliberate is to weigh, to balance, to consider carefully what would be best. To make a mutual promise!

That's the way democracy works. We all have a voice in the deliberation. We come to the table with our concerns and our desires, mindful that others will be there with different—and sometimes conflicting—needs. We can't all have our own way. So, we give a little and we take a little. We win some and we lose some. We carefully weigh and balance everyone's wishes, and in doing so, we reach a compromise—we take a mutual pledge to abide by our decision. And that is good, better, and best for us all.

I think the word *compromise* has been devalued because far too many people are failing to participate in the deliberation. We do not come to the table. We do not speak. We do not vote. Therefore, we're often unhappy with the mutual promises that are made at that table. We feel as if we got stuck with the lint brush! But, we need to be reminded that "It is better to vote than to gripe."

Come to the table. Speak your mind. Listen to others. COMPROMISE.

Good, Better, BEST!

Whenever we would recite our 4-H mantra of motivation, our club leader would add his own words of wisdom: "Remember, you can only do your *best* if you *do good* first."

That's pretty good advice for a democracy.

Just to Get Things Started

ONE MAN'S RUT is another man's ritual.

This is a truth I learned one summer while waiting tables in the coffee shop of a Holiday Inn. Though most of the breakfast customers were travelers and eager to be on their way, Harold was a regular. He was an elderly gentleman, probably a widower, who came in every morning at 7:15, and greeted me with "Hello, old man." I would respond with "How ya' doin', young fella?" and he would laugh, hang up his coat and hat, and sit down at his regular table. We never let any mere itinerant sit there. "Coffee this morning, Harold?" I would ask, and he would nod and say, "Bring a little cow to put in it." Then, he placed his breakfast order. It seldom varied. Sometimes he would have the eggs scrambled instead of poached, but the toast was always wheat and the juice was always orange. But before any of that, Harold would ask for "a side dish of prunes," and with a chuckle and a wink he would add, "just to get things started." That's what kept Harold regular, and for a while, he amused me.

Harold's regularity started to unnerve me after about a month. I would see him coming and I would shudder in dreaded anticipation of "a side dish of prunes, just to get things started." Every morning, "a side dish of prunes, just to get things started." Week after week, "a side dish of prunes, just to get things started." Finally, in an ill-advised

189

attempt to break out of the rut, I greeted Harold one morning with the side dish of prunes already on the table. "There're your prunes, Harold," I said. He didn't look pleased, so I chuckled and winked and added, "just to get things started." He sat down and ate the prunes in silence. I felt miserable, and it took nearly a full week before we were back to normal.

Years later, I became a regular breakfast customer myself at Tony's Cafe. I came in at the same time, sat at the same table, and Dorothy would shout from the counter, "The usual, hon?" I would sit back, relax, and remember Harold. I now knew that it wasn't the prunes that got things started for Harold each morning; it was the routine. It was Harold's morning ritual, and now I had one of my own. It's how I started my day.

We all have our quirks. And our quirks become habits, and our habits become routines, and our routines turn into the rituals that become as sacred as religious traditions. It's how we deal with the passage of time.

Habits are a way of saving time. We do things automatically, without thinking. I didn't have time to study Tony's menu every morning. I had a train to catch. So every morning it was just "the usual, hon." The habit turned into the routine, and Dorothy and I enacted that routine every morning. It wasn't a rut; it was a ritual that evoked the comforting illusion of timelessness. Each morning we reenacted the morning before, and the one before that, and the many mornings back as far as we could remember. It's how we got things started.

Our habits save time.

Our routines preserve time.

Our rituals re-create time.

Our traditions honor time.

When we speak of tradition, we often say, "That's the way we do things." It's our way—our path—it is the road that was forged through the wilderness by our ancestors. By reenacting the rituals of that forging, we start our own journey down that road. Rituals get us started and traditions show us the way. There is an old African proverb that says: "To go back to tradition is the first step forward."

I miss Harold and the Holiday Inn coffee shop. I miss Dorothy and the gang at Tony's. But now every morning I get out of bed, and every morning I scratch the cat's ears, and every morning I say, "Hello, old girl." She stretches and purrs in response, and I like to think she's saying, "How ya' doin', young fella?" Then, we both go downstairs, and while my coffee is brewing, I open the refrigerator, take out the can of Alpo, and asked Angelique, "The usual, hon?"

I don't expect everyone to practice this ritual. All I ask is that you honor and respect its importance to us. It's how we start our day.

In like manner, we need to honor and respect all the ruts, routines, and rituals that people employ as they travel down the road of life. The ruts give them comfort, the routines keep them young, and the rituals remind them that they are not alone. Traditions may be as old as the hills, but we still need them—just to get things started.

I'm Glad You Like It

To compliment or to complement; that is the question.
Whether 'tis nobler at the feast to utter the praise and
*   courtesies of civilized behavior*
Or to speak of debt in the bounty of plenty and by our
*   gratitude perfect it.*

Sorry, Mr. Shakespeare. I had to do it. I've always been fascinated by these two words—*compliment* and *complement*—and somewhat baffled. Why two words when (it seems to me) one would do? As always, I turn to the dictionary for clarification and enlightenment:

USAGE NOTE: *Complement* and *compliment*, though quite distinct in meaning, are sometimes confused because they are pronounced the same. *Complement* means "something that completes or brings to perfection." *Compliment* means "an expression or act of courtesy or praise."

Even with the help of the *American Heritage*, I'm still confused. Are these two words really quite distinct in meaning? I don't think so. I think a "compliment" is a "complement." I think "an expression or act of courtesy or praise" is "something that completes or brings to perfection." In others words, the feast isn't perfect until it's been praised.

193

I've been told that in some cultures it is the belch of the sated guest that signals to the host that the banquet was a success. I prefer the simple but sincere, "That was delicious." Either way, you owe your host that debt of gratitude and praise. Your perfect compliment is the perfect complement to a glorious gift; for that gift has not been truly received until the bearer is unburdened of doubt.

Everyone comes to the feast feeling a little anxious. We worry about how we look and about the gifts we have brought. We hope everyone notices—and appreciates—how much care we've invested in our contribution to the event. We try not to "fish for compliments," but everyone likes to hear words of praise. Then it happens; someone comes up to you and says, "You look great," and now the festivities have begun. It doesn't matter how long you stood in front of your mirror getting ready, the party outfit is not complete until it is reflected in an admirer's eyes.

Too often we're so concerned about hearing the affirming compliment that we fail to notice that someone else is waiting to hear one, too. No matter how self-satisfied another guest may seem, our words of admiration and appreciation can transform the merely magnificent into something quite sublime. As Henry Adams wrote: "He too serves a certain purpose who only stands and cheers." So, *you* may think it's over when the fat lady sings, but it isn't over for *her* until you've leapt to your feet, cheered madly, applauded wildly, and thrown roses onto the stage. Even a diva needs an "Atta Girl!" now and then. That's what you can give to her. And watch how she receives your gift of praise.

There's an art to receiving a compliment gracefully. The diva bows, she curtsies and lifts one rose to clutch to her heart. She rises, looks at you, bows yet again, and smiles humbly as if to say, "I'm glad you like it." In fact, you like it so much that you keep cheering and applauding, and she returns over and over again to the stage. More applause, more cheers, more roses, and more humble bows and smiles. This is fine for a diva. For the rest of us, we should probably keep it to just, "I'm glad you like it." That's all you have to say in response to a compliment: "I'm glad you like it."

Whatever you do, don't throw the courtesy back into your admirer's face. Responding to a compliment with self-deprecating phrases such as: "Oh, this old thing?" or "It was nothing," or "It's just something I threw together" is the kind of false modesty that smells like the bait of someone who is angling for praise. Genuine modesty does not require us to deny our achievements, but only to recognize them ourselves for what they are truly worth. C. S. Lewis once wrote: "The first step toward humility is to realize that one is proud."

We should be proud of our achievements, and we should welcome sincere and measured words of praise. On the other hand, a compliment that outweighs the accomplishment is nothing but empty flattery, and we need to watch out for flatterers. A good teacher once warned me that the person who flatters you for qualities you *don't* have is the same person who will also condemn you for the *faults* you don't have.

A compliment should complement. It should be in exact proportion to the act or object it addresses: "The meal was delicious." "You look lovely." "What a clever thing to say." The response should be "I'm glad you like it."

Or course, something as glorious as the Feast of Existence deserves a lifetime of praise and gratitude. So, to answer the original question: To *compliment* or to *complement?*

> *'tis noblest to complete and perfect our happiness with songs and words of praise.*

Happy Thanksgiving!

It's an Old Family Recipe

FOR MANY YEARS I had this rule about cooking: "If a meal takes longer to prepare than it does to eat, it simply isn't worth it." To spend several hours planning, shopping, and preparing for a meal that could be devoured in just over thirty minutes seemed like inefficient time management. I was very fond of smugly saying, "That's why God created McDonald's."

Eventually, even McDonald's tried my patience. I became a notorious gulper of food, and my rule about *cooking* turned into a rule about *waiting*: "If a Value Meal takes longer to wait for than it does to inhale, it simply isn't worth it." I didn't even park the car. I went through the drive-through line, and I learned to eat an entire Quarter-Pounder with Cheese in less than a dozen bites while driving down an interstate highway. I was so fast that even fast food couldn't keep up with me. Once I actually honked my horn while waiting in line for a milkshake.

This is *not* how to behave at the feast.

Though it is how you behave at a *fast*.

Isn't it curious that we use that same word—*fast*—when we mean "quick," and also when we mean "abstain from food"? Given the second use, "fast food" becomes an oxymoron, doesn't it? Eventually, a steady diet of fast food does seems like eating nothing at all. You find yourself starving. When the next Big Mac Attack hits, you would rather get in the car and drive cross-country for one of Mom's home-cooked meals. You know, one of those meals that takes hours of planning, shopping, and preparation. Such a feast would be worth it.

An Italian man by the name of Carlo Petrini calls these meals *Slow Food* and he maintains that Slow Food is what we truly hunger for—what we are starving for. "Taste is like an umbilical cord," says Petrini, "We all return to our grandmothers, no matter how many detours we take along the way."

In the mid-1980s, just as McDonald's was planning to set up shop in Rome, Petrini launched his crusade for Slow Food and founded the "International Movement for the Defense of and the Right to Pleasure." He penned a manifesto that proclaimed: "We are enslaved by speed. . . . Our defense should begin at the table with Slow Food. . . . May suitable doses of guaranteed sensual pleasure and slow, long-lasting enjoyment preserve us from the contagion of the multitude who mistake frenzy for efficiency." In just over a decade, more than 65,000 people around the world have joined Petrini's Slow Food Movement.

Now, while there is no doubt that I had fallen to "the contagion of the multitude who mistake frenzy for efficiency," and though I'll admit that I was starving for home-cooked food, I still wasn't ready to sign on with Petrini and his dawdling diners. I have this phobia about clubs. But, as I learned more about Slow Food, I found that it isn't a club at all—it's a *Convivium*. *Convivium* is the Latin word for banquet, for drinking, for good company—for *feasting*! Here, at last, at the close of the twentieth century, were

65,000 other people who were concerned about how we behave at the feast!

Imagine—doing good by eating well. That's one of the movement's big projects right now. Petrini believes that Slow Food is as endangered and prone to extinction as any animal or habitat the environmentalists labor to protect. So, he began the Ark Project in a crusade to save those savory foods that definitely take longer to prepare than they do to consume.

I personally think Aunt Annie's cinnamon rolls should go on the Ark. Her recipe calls for potatoes, and the results are simply delicious. She also had a formula for turkey stuffing that I hope wasn't buried with her. We should also save Grandma Currie's coconut cake, Mom's pot roast, and Aunt Opal's macaroni salad. In fact, all of the old family recipes must never be forgotten. And not just the ones for food.

The recipes for good times and good memories are as endangered as the potluck picnic.

Remember this one? "For a truly satisfying feast of story-telling, mix three generations thoroughly and combine them with the old family photo album."

Or, how about this one: "Take one family, several scraps of paper, and an equal number of pencils. Divide the mixture into two teams and start to play Charades. Laugh yourself silly as Grandpa tries to enact *Material Girl* and his granddaughter puzzles over *The Grapes of Wrath*."

The Feast of Existence has taken generations, decades, and centuries to prepare. It's not on the menu at the fast-food court at the shopping mall, and it can't be devoured while speeding along the highway. You have to slow down, pull over, and stop. You have to create an Ark Project all your own. Your have to savor all the old family recipes that will feed and nourish you for a lifetime.

The joy, the caring, and the love is in the preparation. Do good by eating—and living—well.

December

'Tis a Gift

*"All events are secretly interrelated;
the sweep of all we are doing
reaches beyond the horizon
of our comprehension."*

—ABRAHAM JOSHUA HESCHEL

The Chores of Angels

WHEN YOU GROW UP on a farm, the sun rises and sets to the question "Have you finished your chores?" Feeding the chickens. Gathering the eggs. Haying the cattle. Watering the hogs. We all had our chores to do. Twice a day, every day, all year long. And not just farmyard tasks, but also household jobs—making your bed, setting the table, shaking the rugs, folding clothes. No wonder I thought the opening lyrics to the old Christmas hymn were "While shepherds washed their socks at night." I assumed it was one of their chores that had to be done before they went to bed.

So firmly was the work ethic ingrained in my thinking that when, at the age of five, I was given a short rhyme to recite at the church Christmas pageant, I insisted that I would "do it myself." With more than three months of kindergarten phonics under my belt, I sounded out the two-line poem and memorized it in preparation for Christmas Eve. I would accept no help. When my turn came to say my piece, I stood up proudly and said:

Glorious songs from heaven above are sung by angels fair.
The chores of angels fill the night with music on the air.

Choirs—chores. Phonetically, it was an easy mistake to make. What's more, it stands to reason that if the shepherds had their socks to wash, the angels had their chores to do as well. I just wasn't exactly sure what kind of chores would "fill the night with music on the air."

What *are* the chores of angels? What tasks appear on an angel's "To Do" list during this busy time of year? I took a look at some old Christmas carols to see if I could find the answer.

Angels are primarily responsible for three things. We'll start with numbers two and three and get to their number one chore later.

Number two is singing: "Hark, the herald angels sing— sing in exultation—singly sweetly through the night."

Number three is flying: "Wing your flight o'er all the earth"—and occasionally "bend near the earth to touch their harps of gold."

Singing and flying. That's it. Angels sing and fly and everyone refers to them as "Heavenly Hosts." They make it all look so easy. What are their secrets?

I think it starts with the singing. A wise woman once told me, "Angels can fly because they take themselves so lightly." Singing does more than simply make you feel good; it lightens your load. Singing leads to flying—and flying leads to singing.

Singing and flying. If that's all the angels are required to do, what more should we ask of ourselves?

It's easy to get overburdened during the holidays. We make lists, we make promises, and we make plans. We have chores to do, but seldom do these chores "fill the night with music on the air." More often than not, our roster of responsibilities fills the night with anxiety and insomnia. When we should be sleeping, we are scheduling. When we should be dreaming, we are worrying.

We should be singing. We should be flying. We should "lighten up" a little and enjoy the holidays. If it's good enough for the angels, it's good enough for us.

But it's not that easy. Remember, before they get to singing and flying, angels have a number one chore to do. Number one is watching: "While mortals sleep, the angels keep their *watch* of wondering love."

That's the first thing we must do. Watch. Look. See.

The shepherds weren't burning the midnight oil in order to finish their laundry; they were watching. That's why *they* were the first ones the angels came to with the big news. They were watching, waiting, restful but ready for action. They didn't say, "Sorry, Gabriel, I'll be with you as soon as I finish this load." No, they joined in the singing and went with the angels.

We should, too.

We should all limit our holiday list to these three things.

- *Number one.* Watching. Keeping our eyes open to all the good things that are happening.

- *Number two.* Singing. Singing about it. Dancing about it. Touching our harps of gold about it.

- *Number three.* Flying. Lightening up. Unburdening ourselves of a few chores. Do less—not more.

These are the chores of angels.

These are the things we can do to "Fill the night with music on the air!"

Feeling Listless?

Just then there was a strong wind. It blew the list out of Toad's hand. The list blew high into the air. "Help!" cried Toad. "My list is blowing away. What will I do without my list?"

"Hurry!" said Frog. "We will run and catch it."

"No!" shouted Toad. 'I cannot do that."

"Why not?" asked Frog.

"Because," wailed Toad, "running after my list is not one of the things that I wrote on my list of things to do!"

—From *Frog and Toad Together,* by Arnold Lobel

There is both promise and peril in list making. To be liberated with a final triumphant slash of "Done it!" means you must first submit to the enslaving chains of itemization. Any deviation from your written agenda will forge new links that will entangle you forever in the shackles of responsibility. Lists are a joyless, task-oriented way of getting through the holidays.

Remember: "It is a feast to be attended—not a feat to be accomplished."

So why do we insist on making lists? Shopping lists, gift lists, mailing lists, lists of lists. And what *isn't* getting done while we're making our list, checking it twice, and proudly declaring: "Bought it, wrapped it, gave it, planned it, cooked it, served it, wrote it, stamped it, sent it, did it, did it, did it! All done! Fully celebrated at last!"

I made a holiday list last year. The number one directive was to get the Christmas cards out early. Dutifully, I bought the cards, I bought the stamps, and I sat down with my address book to begin. The first name on my list was my dear friend Ethne in London. I hadn't seen her in more than two years, and I owed her a long letter. She had written to me . . . when? Where was that letter from Ethne?

It took some time, but I found her letter—it was dated April 24. I scolded myself for negligence, then sat down to reread her lengthy epistle. The primary nature of our correspondence is to share books we've read, theater we've seen, and places we've visited. Ethne's letter was a treasure trove of recommendations, and I wanted to send to her an equally impressive roster of cultural experiences. I started to search for my stack of theater programs, but this reminded me that I wanted to ask my friend Joanne if she was interested in attending the Shakespeare Festival in Ontario that next summer. I called her immediately.

We discussed the season, decided on what plays we'd like to see, then we talked about possible dates. Of course, I didn't have a calendar yet for the next year, so I told her I would get one, call her back, and we'd make plans.

Whenever I get an engagement book for the new year, I like to go through the current one to jot down any important events that might deserve annual commemoration. This is always a melancholy exercise as I remember and relive the days of the past year. Happy days, frustrating days, days of pleasure and days of loss. There were two devastating deaths that year. I picked up my address book in order to place a gentle "x" and a date next to those names. I flipped through pages and looked for every "x" I had mourned over the years. My tears fell on my unfinished Christmas letter to Ethne.

I picked up my pen to complete the letter, but I couldn't recall the title of one of the books I wanted to tell Ethne about. I perused my jumbled and overstuffed bookshelves and decided it was time to make a donation to the library booksale. As I selected which books to give away, I fanned the pages for the old utility bills, tissues, and canceled checks that I use as bookmarks. To my surprise, I found several photographs that friends had sent, and I thought it might be nice to buy a few inexpensive frames for them. While I was at it, I would frame some of my own snapshots. Now, where were those envelopes of pictures?

Once located, the photographs required several hours of sorting, discarding, and selecting. In the meantime, the books were still unpacked—but, I thought one of the photographs might make a perfect gift for Joanne, which reminded me that we had finally decided on theater dates, and I had to call the box office and take care of that. I went to my desk to find the telephone number—and there was my letter to Ethne—the number one item on my list of things to do. Almost a week had passed and it still wasn't finished.

What had I been doing?

Well, I had done a lot a remembering, I had made some plans for new adventures, and I had shared some personal treasures with friends. All in all, that was a pretty good list of things to do during the holidays. I sat down and finished my letter to Ethne, then I took the boxes of books to the library, shopped for some picture frames, and when I returned home I tore up my list of things to do. It was incredibly liberating and energizing.

I decided the best cure for being listless is being *listless*.

Oh, before I forget, if you haven't read all the *Frog and Toad* books by Arnold Lobel, drop whatever you're doing right now and go get them. You'll find them in the children's section of your local bookstore. They make wonderful gifts. Which reminds me, maybe Ethne would be amused if . . .

Everything Under the Sun

WE COME AT LAST to one of the truly great feasting times of the year, and I don't know what to say. I know what I *want* to say, but I don't know if I should. You can't be too careful these days.

Having been born and raised in a small midwestern farm town, I was totally unprepared for the offense that could be taken when I simply wished someone a "Merry Christmas!"

"I'm Jewish," was the cold response.

"Sorry, I'm not," was my clumsy reply.

The lesson was learned. From then on it was strictly "Happy Holidays" for me. Then, last December, an angry recipient of my generic greeting demanded to know, "What *holidays* are you talking about?" I remained shocked and silent. "Can't you just say Merry Christmas?" he snarled.

As I've been saying, we always have choices. The problem is, this time of year we seem to have too many: Merry Christmas, Happy Hanukkah (or Chanukah?), Feliz Navidad, Seasons Greetings, Happy Holidays, and now Kwanzaa. (If I left anything out, I'm sorry.) But even with all these choices, the odds are you're going to offend someone the moment you open your mouth. "We don't believe in commercial holidays," a puffed-up woman recently told me. At that point my choices were limited to: "Have a nice day" or "Stuff it, lady." I hope she believes in nice days.

Why has it come to this?

Why, at this time of year, when everyone *wants* to celebrate, and when we have so many traditional ways *to* celebrate, why can't we all just, well, *celebrate*? Is this really the time to be so insistent upon our differences?

The American humorist Ambrose Bierce once observed, "Religious tolerance is a kind of infidelity." Maybe that explains it. Maybe people feel as if they're somehow "cheating" on their religious heritage if they fail to assert their faithfulness. Just as someone might turn away an unwanted sexual advance with, "I'm happily married," maybe people refuse the blessing of another faith because they fear it somehow threatens their own. I don't know. As I said, I don't know what to say.

But, I do know what I *want* to say. I want to repeat everything I've said so far. I want us all to come to the feast. I want everyone to feel welcome and to join in a celebration with everyone and with everything we find here. I want us to trust and revel in all the seemingly chaotic richness of this boisterous Everyone's-Invited-Open-House-All-You-Can-Eat-Come-as-You-Are-No-Holds-Barred Feast!

Do you remember the last time I used that phrase? It was in mid-June in reference to the parties of the Great Gatsby. Then we were talking about the longest day of the year—a day of unlimited choices. Now we've come to the *shortest* day of the year. Does this mean our choices are now limited? *NO!* It does not—not unless we *choose* to limit them. Not unless we choose to refuse the blessings that everyone is so eager to share this time of year. If we choose to have a less than "Merry Christmas" because someone else is having a "Happy Hanukkah," then we've made the wrong choice! And vice versa. If the sight of a nativity scene or a menorah can blind us with righteous indignation, then we've reduced our choices to only "Stuff it, lady." How sad!

During these short cold days and long dark nights we come together for warmth, for community, and for the celebration of the seasons. Whether we light candles on our Christmas tree, or on our menorah, or on our solstice wreath, or on whatever we choose, we are all ultimately celebrating the promised return of light. We do this because we all believe that it is better to light those candles than to curse the darkness. How can we then curse anyone's candle? If there is ever a time to celebrate the great, rich, and brilliant illuminating diversity of a Potluck Feast, this surely is it. We should be blinded by the light of our love, not our intolerance.

That is what I want to say—and that is what I *mean* to say—every time I wish someone a "Merry Christmas" or a "Happy Holiday." It is also what I choose to *hear* when someone else blesses me with their holiday greeting.

I have that choice, and I choose to celebrate everything under the sun.

You Are Welcome!

HAVE YOU NOTICED that very few people say "You're welcome" anymore?

Everyone says "Thank you"—but then the other person says "Thank you" right back. And it can go on and on like that. For example, the other day I was shopping at the stationery store for holiday gifts. I made my selections, then went to the counter, where I handed them to the clerk. "Thank you," she said. "Are you ready to check out?"

"Yes, thank you," I replied.

She told me the total of my purchase and I thanked her for that information as I handed her some cash. She thanked me. When she gave me my change, I thanked her. She put my gifts into a shopping bag, handed it to me, and thanked me once again, and I thanked her right back. As I left she said, "Thank you, come again." "Thank you, I will," I replied.

Nine "Thank yous," and not once did I feel welcomed.

It happens all the time. It reminds me of those terribly polite little cartoon chipmunks named Chip and Dale. Do you remember them? Their dialogue usually ran something like this:

"After you."

"No, after *you*."

"No, I insist—after you!"

"Well, thank you."

"No, thank *you*."

"Really, you are too kind."

"No, it is you who are kind."

"Thank you."

"No, thank *you!*"

It just never ends. What's intended to be a grateful acceptance, "Thank you," gets turned into a kind of rejection: "No, thank you." I know it's supposed to be polite, and I know this is a book about good behavior, but it's not polite when our niceties are reduced to thoughtless babble.

On the other hand, the reverse never happens. When someone greets you at their front door and says, "Welcome to our home," you would never reply with, "Oh, no—welcome *you!*" You would say, "Thank you." It's good to say "Thank you." But it's also good to hear—and to *know*—that "You're welcome."

What does it mean when we say the words "You're welcome"?

It means, "You are gladly and cordially received; freely and willingly permitted." Or more simply put, "I'm glad you are here!" That much is commonly understood. But "You're welcome" is also used in response to "Thank you," and *then* it means, "You're under no obligation for the favor given."

You are welcome! You're under no obligation for the favor given! But the catch is, "You're welcome" is used in *response* to "Thank you."

In other words, you're not going to hear "You're welcome" unless you say "Thank you" first. Remember, you always have a choice about how you are going to behave—about how you are going to respond. So if you want to feel welcome—if you want to sing and celebrate at the Feast of

Existence, then start saying "Thank you" to life and all it has to offer.

Say "Thank you" for the bounty, and say it for every crowded table and hurried day.

Say "Thank you" for all of the fellow guests and for the many and varied gifts they share. Say it when someone says, "Pull up a chair."

Say "Thank you" for the work you do—and for the work others do for you.

Say "Thank you" for the mistakes you learn from, and say "Thank you" for the regrets you send away.

Say "Thank you" for the dreams, and "Thank you" for the songs.

Say "Thank you," and know that "You are welcome!"

We come as guests to the Feast of Existence, and it is only right for us to say "Thank you." But just as importantly, we need to know "You're welcome." We need to know it in our hearts and we need to hear it from, and we need to say it to, each other.

"You're welcome." You are gladly and cordially received.

"You're welcome." You are freely and willingly permitted.

"You're welcome." You are under no obligation—except to be joyous.

You are welcome. Be glad you are alive.

That's the best way to behave at the feast!

"Thank you" for listening!

And "You are welcome!"

ACKNOWLEDGMENTS

I WAS BORN on my mother's birthday.

I mention this now only because I want to talk about being unexpected. Not that I was unexpected; Mom obviously knew I was coming—but she didn't know I would arrive on her birthday. That was a surprise. "The best birthday surprise I ever got," she always tells me. And that has made all the difference.

When you start out life as an unexpected, but lovingly welcomed, surprise, you want to re-create that scenario for a lifetime. Unexpected—but welcomed—and dubbed "the best."

You knock on a lot of doors—and a few of them are slammed in your face—but eventually, someone extraordinary welcomes you into his or her life and it's the *best* thing that ever happened. Soon, you hear knocking at your own door, and standing at the threshold is an unexpected guest. Life has taught you to trust in surprises, so you open the door, say "Welcome," and the feast begins.

There are many such "guests" I want to acknowledge for my own personal celebration of the feast. In each case, either I came as an unexpected guest to their door, or they came to mine—but either way, we welcomed one another. Each time it was *the best* thing that ever happened to me.

So, I start off with Mom and Dad, Mr. and Mrs. Wilbur

219

Currie, and my siblings, Daryl Currie, Diane Tapper, and Darlene Raveling. I was the last to arrive, and they all made me feel as if the family feast was a party being thrown just for me. There's a difference between being "spoiled" and being lovingly nurtured to mature "ripeness." Every kid should have this kind of beginning.

Next, Jean Hogue. When I was only five or six years old, I tagged along with my mother to Jean's house, where I sat down at her piano and started to pick out a few tunes by ear. Jean never expected to be my piano teacher, but she welcomed me as her student and started me on a lifetime of loving music. She was the first of many wonderful teachers who graced my life with a love of music, theater, and books.

My love of theater led me to Joanne Garraway. I was a stranger in a strange town until I saw a newspaper notice concerning the local community theater. Unexpectedly, it took me to Joanne's door, where I received one of the warmest welcomes of my life. She has been my friend for nearly twenty years, and at least once a month for all those years she has insisted, "You should be writing."

My love of books led me to Jack Coleman. What booklover hasn't dreamed of owning a bookstore on the village green in a small Vermont village? Without Jack, that dream would've never come true. When we met, quite unexpectedly, he was, appropriately, the quintessential innkeeper. He opened his door and his heart, and we set up shop.

Through the door of that bookshop came Justine Rendal, who in turn introduced me to the novelist Olivia Goldsmith. I learned a lot from both of them. At least three times a week for more than two years either Justine or Olivia would telephone very early in the morning to ask,

"Are you writing?" If Justine was calling we talked about *my* writing; if Olivia was calling we talked about *hers*. Either way, I couldn't have done it without their lessons in persistence.

That persistence led to the door of Mary Evans. I arrived as an unexpected manuscript on her desk, and she welcomed me. It was her generosity of spirit coupled with an amazing savvy that brought this book to life. As agent extraordinaire, Mary knocked on the right door, and Diane Reverand at HarperCollins enthusiastically said, "Come on in!" She wasn't expecting me either, but her welcome could not have been more genuine, warm, and caring.

Somewhere along the way came Michael Kohlmann. I'm not sure who knocked on whose door, but the party began the day we met. He is, without a doubt, the very best unexpected guest and companion I will ever know. He is welcome by virtue of being indispensable. That's what I like the best about him.

There are so many others: Jane Cox, Kurt Halstead, Jeanne and Michael Shafer, Steve Rubin, Ed Town, Leo Graham, Mitzi Hakey, Janis Karanza, Diana Toomey—I feel like an Oscar winner who is about to be cut off with the theme music, so at the risk of leaving someone out, I'll stop.

Life has taught me to welcome the unexpected guest— always to have an extra place set at the table, and always to find room for the stranger at the inn. It's the knock at the door that can turn the ordinary meal into the feast.

Of course, now I'm knocking at *your* door, and I guess if you've read this far, you've decided to let me in. So, I want to thank *you,* too.